THE MASTER TEACHERS
AND
THE ART OF TEACHING

PITMAN EDUCATION SERIES

Rychard Fink, General Editor

JOHN E. COLMAN, C.M.

St. John's University

THE MASTER
TEACHERS AND THE
ART OF TEACHING

PITMAN PUBLISHING CORPORATION

NEW YORK   TORONTO   LONDON

PARTRIDGE

ACKNOWLEDGMENTS

My special thanks go to Miss Patricia Tunison, whose dedicated work and ability as a writer have made this volume possible.

I am also indebted to Robert S. Ulich and the Harvard University Press for permission to use selections from Confucius and Descartes in *Three Thousand Years of Educational Wisdom;* The New American Library of World Literature, Inc., for permission to use a section of Plato's *Symposium* in a Mentor Book, *Great Dialogues of Plato,* translated by W. H. D. Rouse; D. C. Heath and Company for the use of material from John Dewey's *How We Think;* Current History, Inc., for the use of material of John Dewey's article, "The Need for Orientation," in the former magazine, *Forum and Century;* The Macmillan Company for permission to use material from John Dewey's *Democracy and Education;* and Mrs. William Heard Kilpatrick for permission to use material from William Heard Kilpatrick's *Foundations of Method.*

In addition to my gratitude to Miss Tunison and the authors and publishers mentioned, I would be remiss if I did not acknowledge my deep debt of thanks to Reverend John B. Murray, C.M., and Miss Margaret E. Courtney who encouraged me to complete the work, read the manuscript with critical attention, and made excellent suggestions for its improvement.

Finally, the entire volume was efficiently and expertly prepared for the publisher by Miss Carol Kollmer, to whom I shall be forever grateful.

For any errors of fact or interpretation, of course, I am fully responsible and beg the reader's indulgence.

JOHN E. COLMAN, C.M.

To my Mother and Father—
Master Teachers

CONTENTS

THE MASTER TEACHERS
AND
THE ART OF TEACHING

DO YOU WANT
TO BE A BETTER TEACHER?

---

*How are we going to get the best education
in the world? One of the ways is to have the
best trained teachers.* JOHN F. KENNEDY

The crucial significance of our late President Kennedy's declaration is reechoed more strongly every September as school bells ring and thousands of Americans embark on a new career—they begin to teach. The moment these new teachers walk to the front of their classrooms to face their students, they are confronted with the same problem that has challenged educators for many centuries—how to teach.

Teachers today must not only be adept as instructors, but they should be eager learners themselves. They also must be good leaders, listeners, coaches, confidantes, and, yes, even expert milk-money collectors and recordkeepers. As human beings thus charged by society with so many responsibilities, teachers must indeed be many-faceted.

Such a multidimensional role requires genuine dedication to the principles of educational excellence. One can begin to learn about this task of being a teacher by trying to understand the meaning of the word "education." Unfortunately, too many people have the erroneous impression that the word is from the Latin *educo, educere,* meaning "to draw forth or to lead out of."

To carry that concept of education into the classroom

would mean that the teacher is one who elicits answers in much the same way that a dentist extracts teeth. But a teacher is not a dentist, and education should not be thought of only from that point of view.

Education is more than merely asking students to give back what the teacher has presented. "Education" truly means "to nourish" (from the Latin *educo, educare*). Consequently, one might envision the role of the teacher as similar to that of a young mother fondling her child at her breast. Just as the mother gives the child some of her substance necessary for the child's growth, so teachers must nourish their students with the principles of learning and living. Once it is agreed that teaching is not merely an encyclopedic transmittal of facts, the vital question still remains *how* one may most effectively teach the values and concepts of life.

Just as there is no one best road to Loch Lomond, so too there is no single success formula for teachers to follow. Although opinions vary whether teachers are "born" or "made," the author of this volume subscribes to the notion that the best teachers cannot be classified in either category exclusively. Innate skill and talent are certainly the prerequisites of a good teacher, but such ability must be thoroughly developed and enhanced with the knowledge of "how to teach" before one can be truly successful in the classroom.

The chapters that follow are intended to help educators improve and grow in the use of their natural capacities by the presentation of a diversified and challenging collection of techniques or methods.

It is also hoped that this volume will have particular value for students of education who are preparing to teach. This compilation might serve additionally as a guide for some collegians who may be called upon to teach either their classmates or in a training program in their future employment.

From the parents in ancient Hebrew times to the modern

masters in nongraded schools, teaching methods as varied and distinctive as the chronology of mankind which produced our educational heritage have evolved. Although the author attempts to scan the centuries and focus briefly on the best attributes of each method of teaching, it is not expected that the reader will choose only one method which seems most sound to him and then adopt it. Rather it is recommended that many ideas and techniques might be drawn from this compilation and then synthesized into an effective and flexible overall teaching program. Some methods fit some situations better than others. A discerning and dutiful teacher will test, evaluate, and finally select the technique that will most effectively convey his particular message to a certain group of learners. It is the teacher with such a variety of methodology who is best prepared to meet the daily challenge of reaching other minds.

The format of this volume is intentionally uniform. After a brief chapter which gives a general approach to the problem of teaching, the author has tried to follow this simple outline for each chapter: (1) a brief historical description of the specific method as it was originally practiced; (2) a functional outline of the ideal use and effectiveness of this technique; and (3) a summary incorporating some significant advantages and/or limitations of the method.

The fundamental reason for this gathering together of pertinent data on the subject of how to teach arises from the apparent paucity of good material in this field. Previous studies of this nature may be divided roughly into two categories: (1) those written about the time of the First World War, which show a definite bias of the author toward one or the other of the methods employed; and (2) current works in the field of education, which seem to cover every item that the teacher should know . . . except how to teach. Usually even books that bear this title are devoted to the incidentals of classroom management such as lighting, heat, fresh air, and recordkeeping. While trivial in relation to the total teaching program, these details are not to be slighted by the teacher. They are conducive to the overall atmosphere or "where" of good learning, but in this volume we shall be restricted primarily to the methods or "how" of teaching.

1. THE GENERAL APPROACH

And so . . . teach!

Someone who plans a trip from New York to California has the choice of determining the means he wishes to use to reach his destination. He may, for example, travel by train, plane, boat, automobile, horseback, bicycle, or on foot.

In educational language, the goal of the trip can be termed the "aim" and the means adopted the "method." It is not our purpose here to discuss the various "aims" of education. Such considerations may be found elsewhere.

The methods of the teacher, however, are the vital means by which each day's learnings are conveyed to the students. Though described simply as an orderly procedure to obtain a desired end, method is more than that. Methods in education would be totally unrealistic if the need of the student and the particular scope of the course content were ignored. Thus, an appropriate definition of method might be the following: "An ordered system by which a teacher puts educative agents to work on humans to produce certain changes or results."

Now just as the best way of going from New York to California would be determined by an individual's personal preferences and resources, so also a teacher's choice of methods in education is contingent on many factors. The ability of the teacher to use a particular method, the capacity of the class to comprehend by that method, and the adaptability of the subject matter to that specific method are crucial considerations which a teacher must evaluate to determine the methodology he chooses.

Many of the methods to be presented in this book may initially appear sterile or inert, but each one has had a champion in former times, and, moreover, each method is capable of achieving desirable changes or results if the vital force of the teacher is added to make the method come to life.

It is strongly recommended to the beginning teacher that he designate in his plan book the particular method which he employed in presenting a lesson. His evaluation of its success may be determined after the first time the subject was taught.

Another way of phrasing the same recommendation is to suggest that a particular teacher may not be adept at handling a specific method, that certain material may not lend itself to that method, or that the class may not be capable of absorbing the material when presented in that particular way. The Scholastic adage, *Experientia docet*, is applicable only if the teacher really learns that the subject matter was or was not conveyed by the use of a particular method.

Basically, once the method has been selected a teacher ought to include five elements in every lesson: aim, introduction, content, summary, and evaluation.

1. *Aim.* The *aim*, first of all, should be a specific objective for each class. If a teacher does not have a special aim for a particular class, the class will suffer, no matter what method is used to try to teach these students.

A teacher's aim should not be the general goals which he hopes to accomplish in a subject area for a semester or whole year, but rather his precise purpose for that one hour of class. An example would be the French teacher whose aim for a class hour is the teaching of the principal parts of four irregular verbs. He would not intend to teach the whole French language, but only that which it is possible to cover well in one hour. Another illustration would be the mathematics teacher who should attempt to teach only the properties of an equilateral triangle in one lesson, rather than try to explain the whole scope of geometry. Although the teacher's method in accomplishing his aim could be the lecture method, the memorization method, the discussion method, or any of the others, the important thing is that the teacher is aware of a *specific* purpose in that particular class.

It is true that the class itself might deviate from the expressed aim of the teacher, and, in actual practice, far different aims may be realized—sometimes better than the original conception—but the rule to be followed is that there should be at least one specific aim for each class period.

2. *Introduction.* The second major ingredient which may be expected in every lesson is the *introduction.* Whether it be elaborately long or concisely brief, the introduction should primarily serve as a tie-in with material of a previous lesson or experience.

Just as a television set must be warmed up and tuned in before the picture appears, so students must be put in the proper focus before the lesson can reach all clearly.

This conditioning of students to stimuli for favorable reaction to material about to be presented is called *mind set.* By a meaningful and vivid introduction, the teacher thus sets students' minds on the topic and prepares them to receive and understand the principles about to be conveyed.

3. *Content.* Every lesson must have substance or *content.* This is the message or subject matter the teacher wishes to convey by his chosen methods. Whether it be the principle of the inclined plane or spelling words with similar roots, the content is the essence of the lesson.

The teacher must appreciate that the content which he plans to impart in a particular class period should be limited in scope and tailored to the abilities and attention span of the students.

If a beginning teacher does not realize that the pupils are able to absorb only a limited amount of subject matter in a given hour, he will soon learn this from experience. Students should not go unchallenged, however, and a teacher should never lower his standards concerning the material which he wishes to accomplish throughout a course. On the other hand, a teacher must recognize that a little content well absorbed will achieve more toward his ultimate goal than a great quantity of material which is presented to a class but is beyond its comprehension.

4. *Summary.* A *summary* is also important in the learning process. As a reenforcement of the principles already taught, repetition which summarizes the lesson's content helps the students to retain the subject matter.

There are many means of refreshing minds by repetition; correlated readings and assignments frequently give students further insight into the material. A teacher's summary, which should come at the end of each class, also often clarifies and illumines vital points for the students. Of course, frequent and well-spaced reviews, with the pupils contributing in an active way, are the most common means of satisfying this need for repetition.

5. *Evaluation.* The final step for each teacher's class is some form of *evaluation.* This evaluation may be given at the end of each period to the entire class in a test form, or the basic questions may be posed in general and students selected at random to answer.

This form of evaluation serves not so much to see if the students are exactly correct, but rather to ascertain if the class has grasped the basic principles presented.

A brief digest of the general approach that is expected in every one of the methods which follow may be depicted in this way.

Every lesson needs *five* elements:
1. *aim*—specific
2. *introduction*—tie-in
3. *content*—subject matter
4. *summary*—repetition
5. *evaluation*—success(?)

2. THE MEMORIZATION
METHOD

The Ancient Hebrews made sure, and so did the Spartans.

Let us try to picture for ourselves what it was like many centuries ago in the land of Palestine. As the cool breezes of what we can imagine to be March 8, 1492 B.C. sweep over the canvas which separates them from the blue Mediterranean sky, a Hebrew father cautions his son, to whom we will give the name David, to listen closely to the *Shema.*

"Now, little David, repeat after me. 'Hear, O Israel, the Lord thy God is One God.'"

"Yes, father. 'Hear, O Israel . . . Israel . . . Israel . . . the . . . the . . .'"

"David, I told you to pay attention! Now, once again, 'Hear, O Israel, the Lord thy God is One God.'"

"'Hear, O Israel, the Lord thy God is . . . is . . . One God!'"

"Yes, but you must practice over and over and do better tomorrow, David, or else I shall have to punish you."

On the next evening in the same setting: "Little David, stand up and tell me what you learned yesterday."

"Yes, father. . . . 'Hear, O Israel, the Lord thy God is One God.'"

*"Well done! You have mastered your lesson, my son,
and now for the next passage. Listen closely. . . ."*

The preceding dialog illustrates the teaching technique
known as the memorization method. The ancient Hebrews
used this method of rote memory, and we in the twentieth
century still imitate their practices.

It is true that these tribes of nomadic herdsmen who
cultivated the soil and grazed their flocks in Palestine could
not provide schools for their children as we know them
today. Nevertheless, the education of the youngsters was not
neglected.

Not only did these ancient Hebrew fathers meticulously
transmit the teachings of the Law of Yahweh to their sons
and daughters, but all other subjects, such as astronomy and
history, were explained and related in the home, with the
basic aim of making the Hebrew youths into persons pleasing to God.

With the father recounting the noteworthy events, each
child memorized verbatim while the family gathered at the
close of the day in the tent or mud-brick hut which was
home. The children were expected to repeat perfectly what
the father had said on the previous night; otherwise the
Hebrew parent would punish the youth. (It is also interesting to note that the Hebrew word *shanah* which is usually
translated as "to teach" might just as easily be translated
"to repeat.") As the prescription of Proverbs reads, "Spare
the rod, and thou art no friend to thy son" (Proverbs 13:24).

Although there is little room for deviation in the rote
method, the Hebrews were successful with this method
because of their intense fidelity to the Word of God. Theirs
was a theocratic society fundamentally based on discipline
and the relationship of the Hebrew to his God.

If one is tempted to reject this method, believing it to be
practical only for teaching religion, then perhaps a glance

at another civilization might be taken. A very different content of education was advocated by the early Spartans in
accordance with their aim of developing courage, military
skill, and obedience to law and custom. In using the rote
method to an unpleasant extreme, these Greeks allowed no
individual freedom of thought and required strict imitation
and memorization of everything from simple chants to
physical exercises.

Although these Spartans (c. 750 to 150 B.C.) shared the
Greek language and the Homeric poems with their Athenian
cousins, they placed little emphasis upon an intellectual
education. In fact, only healthy youngsters who potentially
could best serve the state were "permitted" by the elders to
live.

Once a child's existence was approved, he remained at
home until he was seven years old. After that point he was
sent to a barracks-type boarding school where he was placed
under the supervision of an *eiren*, a young man about twenty
years old who was responsible for the education of the
youths entrusted to him. Once at school Spartan youths
learned, by strict imitation and rote memorization, the simple Doric chants and dances, the patriotic songs, the methods
of foraging for food and firewood, and the physical exercises
of the *ilai* (the Greek word used to describe a pack of youths,
from seven to eighteen years of age, to which the particular
child was assigned).

As in Hebrew practice, failure of a Spartan child to memorize correctly brought a penalty of strict punishment. Not
only the *eiren* but any senior citizen could punish the lads
of the pack; this punishment was not merely a simple tap,
but a whipping or even a flogging. It must be pointed out,
however, that this punishment was not the essence of the
rote method of teaching. The method itself was the imitation and memorization, while the punishment was only a
means to insure the effectiveness of the method.

Insofar as the Spartans developed a strong citizenry

inculcated with an authoritarian devotion to the state, they did truly succeed as teachers in their use of the rote method. However, later ages have regarded their philosophy of "the citizen is for the state—not the society for the individual" as one of the causes of their downfall.

The memorization method itself, however, has long outlived its early practitioners by many centuries. In fact, this technique of teaching even can be seen during the dawn of civilization on the North American continent.

The proficiency of the American Indians in their use of the memorization method of instruction was evident as the Indian chief would repeatedly demonstrate to his son the best technique of killing a bison with a bow and arrow. The young brave would carefully imitate his father's actions until his lesson in hunting was well mastered. An Indian maiden would similarly spend long hours watching her mother prepare the maize for dinner. After repeating the requirements of the squaw's recipe day after day, the young girl would soon be well versed in that particular cooking skill.

Like the Hebrews and Spartans, the American Indians, by carefully instilling in their young the principles they held dear, were successful as teachers, but for different reasons. The Ancient Hebrews relied on the theocratic core of their educational practices, while the Spartans depended on the subservience of the individual to the state, and the Indians were motivated by their need to survive in the wilderness. Despite these different situations, however, the three groups depended on the memorization method for the success of their educational process, and all three contributed significantly to the development of this method.

Of all the methods of teaching, the one upon which the most abuse is usually heaped is this method of repetition or memorization. Actually, this method has enjoyed the longest period of use, and a teacher who is trying to improve should be able to summon this technique from his "bag of tricks."

Before we delve into the most effective uses of the memorization method in modern education, let us first distinguish between rote and logical memory.

Rote memory is a mechanical memorization which requires that symbols rather than ideas be learned verbatim. A youngster's recitation of the alphabet or the multiplication tables would be illustrations of rote memory exercises.

Logical memory is a rational memorization involving a meaningful understanding of principles to be mastered. An example of logical memory in action might occur when a teacher asks his class to memorize four fundamental principles of education. They should be committed to memory and understood by all who wish to teach:

1. Education is not the same as schooling.
2. Education is preparation for the age in which it is given.
3. Education is necessarily an individual experience.
4. Education is preparation for total responsibility.

In past ages rote or mechanical memorization was stressed excessively, whereas the comprehension of the material was somewhat neglected.

The good teacher, however, will be careful not to exclude rote learning merely because there was an overemphasis on it in the past, but will realize the method's utility, even its necessity, in twentieth-century America. No matter what his educational philosophy may be, the teacher frequently finds it necessary to plan for drill and memorization experiences. The question should not be whether drill or memorization are important. The basic concern should be for the most helpful kind of drill and memorization.

Just as the Hebrew child learned passages of the Scriptures verbatim from his father and the Spartan youth memorized selections from Homer and Hesiod, so also the American youth of today must learn verbatim certain tables of mathematics, specific selections of prose and poetry, occasional definitions, important principles, governing laws, and thousands of spelling words.

The child first uses rote memory in these matters until, as he matures, the rote method may be abandoned and replaced by logical memory. Spelling provides us with an excellent example of the rote method in operation. After all, what is spelling but the grouping of specific letters fitted together to form words? One way to learn how to spell is either to sound out the words or to memorize the order in which the letters are properly combined to give us the accurate spelling.

Learning of foreign languages also means using rote memorization to master verb endings, noun forms, and idiomatic expressions. The learning of a list of presidents in American history, the state capitals in geography, or a set of geometric theorems are also typical situations for this method of imitation.

Logical memorization, on the other hand, presupposes rational understanding of the concepts involved. In this type of memory work, the reasoning powers play a very important role, and logical association shows cause and effect. This naturally requires an analysis of the subject matter, a recognition of significant features and their relation to each other as well as to other experiences of the learner. Poetry, for example, after being committed to memory, should then be analyzed and studied for its message to be truly appreciated and understood. A person must comprehend what it means to be "contrary" before he can really glean enjoyment from a recitation of "Mary, Mary, quite contrary, / How does your garden grow?"

Now the question arises as to how the memorization method may be best presented in a learning situation. Whether intended for rote or logical mastery, such subject matter should be presented in a pattern of four steps termed "The Four R's": Reflection + Repetition + Recitation = Retention.

Reflection upon the material—whether in the Hebrew home, the Spartan barracks, the Indian wigwam, or the American classroom—means actual attention to the subject matter being memorized.

By *repetition,* the material, like the famous ABC rhyme of ancient vintage—or the more recent "Do, Re, Me" verse in *The Sound of Music*—is reiterated over and over until the pupil has grasped it.

The *recitation* of the content, like the performance given by the Hebrew children each evening for their father, serves as a self-test to determine if there are any aspects of the material which have not been fully mastered.

The final product or result of the memory cycle should be *retention,* which is achieved when the subject matter—whether it be the spelling of a word or a principle of education—is permanently committed to memory.

SUMMARY

It is quite likely that this notion of the use of the memory as a method in learning may horrify some prospective members of the teaching profession. Although these individuals may ideally view the real purpose of trying to be a teacher as exclusively cultivating the intellect of the pupil, they will soon discover that the classroom situation, as well as the everyday necessities of life, demand that everyone must "remember" special facts, events, formulas, and expressions.

The many opportune times for remembered or memorized information will not only insure that one knows such facts as "the great educator, Juan Luis Vives, was born in 1492," but will also provide many starting points for a good lesson. For example, once a teacher is certain that his pupils know the words of a new poem, only then may proper interpretation of the verse be attempted. Likewise, exercises in written communication cannot be initiated until the proper sequence of the twenty-six letters in the alphabet is memorized.

The chief disadvantage of the memory method is, of course, that it naturally limits freedom of thought and creativity. Like all methods of teaching, however, the rote method is invaluable if it is employed when its features of imitation and repetition are most beneficial to the learner.

The best rule to *remember* about the memory method (and every method, for that matter) is that there is much merit in using it as part of a teacher's repertoire when the subject matter and situation are compatible to memorization, but to rely on this method exclusively can be stifling to the questioning minds of learners.

3. THE LECTURE METHOD

Now, gentlemen . . .

It is probably true that the word "lecture" connotes more unpleasant recollections on the part of students than any other single term in the English language. There is an almost automatic cringe associated with it, a yawn that must be stifled and a fear of boredom that borders on nausea.

Yet in educational circles today, the lecture method of learning is second only to the memorization method in popular use. Like the memory method, the lecture was being used to teach long before Christ. In fact, in ancient China we discover some of the earliest forms of this method in practice.

As a people espousing deep reverence for the ideas and customs of the past, the Chinese placed great emphasis on instilling an appreciation of their culture in their children. Not only was this heritage of ancestral virtue stressed in the home, but the Chinese also established a formal system of schooling in every village.

Among the renowned teachers who labored to instruct the people in the wisdom of the ancients was Confucius (551-?479 B.C.), often called the "inspiration of the Chinese system of education." Confucius' words and works have profoundly affected Oriental learning to this day.

Although reverence for parents living or dead was the keynote of Confucius' teaching, he also spoke or "lectured" to his fellow men on the corresponding importance of learning and knowledge in order to cherish the past fully and to be a good citizen in the present. In fact, he frequently stressed the vital role of education in the progress of culture. "The three kings and the four dynasties were what they were by their teachers."[1]

It is not difficult to visualize Confucius lecturing on the principles of life under the roof of a simple wooden building in the great valley of the Yangtze. Confucius would speak in a sermonlike way, using aphorisms and sage sayings to convey philosophical and moral lessons to the people. His delivery was not merely the reading of a text or a set of laws, but rather the spontaneous and heartfelt giving of advice of a wise teacher.

Listen for a moment as Confucius gives a few pointers on good teaching:

> The good singer makes men able to continue his notes, and so the good teacher makes them able to carry out his ideas. His words are brief, but far-reaching; unpretentious, but deep; with few illustrations, but instructive. In this way he may be said to perpetuate his ideas.[2]

So successful was Confucius as a teacher that long after his death he was worshiped as one of the sacred ancestors and benefactors of the nation. Although today we would call his method the "lecture," in the days of this great Chinese thinker such terminology did not exist.

It was not until many centuries later in the Middle Ages of Western Europe that the "lecture method" began to assume its modern connotations. This was the period before the printing press, when books were still a treasure. Consequently, since the teacher in the medieval universities was

---

[1] Confucius, *Hsio Ki*, or, *Record on the Subject of Education*, Book XVI, 16 as found in Robert Ulich (Ed.), *Three Thousand Years of Educational Wisdom* (Cambridge, Mass.: Harvard University Press, 1954), p. 22.

[2] *Ibid.*

usually the only one who possessed a book, the students just listened and took notes as the teacher read the text aloud.

Of course, this is not what we would describe as a good lecture. Nevertheless, the habit of reading to the students from a single textbook became synonymous with this method of teaching. The Latin word *lego* (*legere, lectus*), which means "to read," was generalized to mean "to teach," and this dictation-type of instruction was labeled "the lecture method."

A visit to the University of Salerno in 1220 A.D. will illustrate this form of the lecture method in action. Here we see a professor lecturing on anatomy.

"Now, gentlemen, today we shall learn about the functions of the skeletal system. We shall refer to the works of the Greek writers Hippocrates (*c.* ?460-?377 B.C.) and Galen (*c.* 164 A.D.) and to those of the Jewish physician Asaph ben Berechiah (*c.* ?650 A.D.).

"I shall now read the first selection to you . . ."

Although the professors at Salerno occasionally used their own words and writings, it was usually the custom to quote at length from a variety of sources in presenting each day's lessons. Consequently, about all the students were assured of at the end of a course at the university level were their own personal notebooks which closely resembled today's annotated editions.

It has also been said that in many instances, unfortunately, the words of the teacher's reading or "lecture" went to the notes of the student without passing through the minds of either. As a method of teaching, this form of lecture truly left much to be desired.

The invention of movable type at Mainz, Germany, by Johann Gutenberg in the 1430's, and the subsequent availability of books helped to correct the abuses of the lecture method. European and American universities had come very far in this regard by the beginning of the present century.

For instance, a lecture at the University of Ireland

in 1920 on the *filid* (learned poets) would presuppose that the students had all read the chapter in their textbook dealing with this phase of Celtic literature. The professor's lecture would therefore be based on his interpretations of the chapter as well as on other literature on the topic. He occasionally read a few lines of a passage for emphasis, but his discourse was mainly his own ideas delivered in his own terms, which were geared for the particular group of students before him.

This gradual development of the lecture method, from the little sermons or aphorisms of Confucius through the period of reading a textbook verbatim for the students' transcription into notes to the modern conception of a lecture, has been marred by much misuse and many erroneous practices.

Nevertheless, as can be said of all methods, once a suitable teaching situation and form of content are present, the proper utilization of a specific method can lead to a most successful lesson. The lecture method is certainly no exception to this rule.

An oral exposition or instruction of facts or principles by a teacher is usually referred to as the *lecture method*. While it is a common practice in many educational ranks today to deride the lecture (principally because of its misuse), there can be little doubt that it will long continue to be one of the methods most frequently used by the teacher—and rightly so!

Our main concern here is to set guidelines for the most skillful use of this method in the modern classroom. It must be stressed that learners have been taught efficiently for many centuries by good speeches, sermons, talks, or "lectures." Such discourses, however, are usually not just read, but delivered—truly animating the spoken word to impress the listeners.

Reading a text is not teaching, but explaining, interpreting, and elaborating on the ideas and concepts published therein, so that others may comprehend the principles, can result in a good lecture.

Once the lecturer has decided upon his topic, he is faced with the initial task of accumulating the required information. It is extremely important that he explore his own mind before consulting any other source. Doing creative thinking gives the teacher a chance to conceive of a fresh, original approach, not one drawn from the thoughts of others.

The lecturer must also determine the point of view from which the subject is to be presented. Writing down at random any facts touching on the topic helps him to amass a group of ideas with which to start. After this he can go to standard reference works for more complete information. This approach, coupled with his own creative thinking, helps the teacher to develop a perspective on the subject. Then comes the second phase of his preparation period, equally as important as the first: He must tailor the lecture to his hearers. Neither half is sufficient without the other.

Generally speaking, after this preliminary preparation, five steps are required in the formal lecture of today.

1. *Definition of terms* is the teacher's explanation of the vocabulary, expressions, or symbols that will be basic to the proper understanding of the concepts he presents. Before teaching the functions of the tooth, the professor at the University of Salerno first defined a tooth as "a hard body in the mouth attached to the skeleton, developed from the dermis or true skin."

Similarly, the teacher in a modern elementary school who attempts to develop a creative-writing lesson on the topic "If I Had a Money Tree" must first make certain that the children understand the concept of a tree. The youngsters must also know the uses and values of money before they can be expected to visualize a "money tree."

2. *Division and subdivision of details* comprise the second phase of the lecture. This step requires the teacher to break down the general terms or concepts into their simplest component parts and segments.

Just as the medieval professor would have divided his explanation of the tooth into the enamel, the dentine, and the cementum, so also the teacher of today's Money Tree Lesson would be obliged to discuss the roots, trunk, branches, stems, and leaves of the tree as well as the forms and functions of money.

3. *The summary* at this point in the lecture is a recapitulation, which condenses and repeats the principal aspects of the lesson thus far. This helps the pupils to select and take note of the salient features of the information presented, rather than trying to write a running commentary of everything the teacher has discussed. The summary should be concise, yet logical and correlated.

4 and 5. The final two steps are the *raising* and *solving of objections* which provide an opportunity for the teacher to answer questions, clarify misunderstandings, or perhaps redefine the significance of a certain term in relation to the total comprehension of the topic being discussed. "In what part of the tooth does decay begin" might have been the query of a University of Salerno student, whereas today's fourth grader may wonder, "Do money trees really grow?" After these difficulties are resolved for the students, the lesson is complete.

SUMMARY

In perusing the five steps of a good lecture, it is fairly evident that this lecture method actually embraces many methods in its overall scope: there is some rote, a little discussion, and part disputation as well. The achievement of the total lecture method itself therefore requires much skill and versatility in addition to a learning situation conducive to the general approach of a discourse.

Once it is successfully rendered, a good lecture has many premiums. It is economical with precious classroom time because it brings the teacher's ideas into immediate focus. It also readily utilizes the teacher's experience and savoir-faire, rather than allowing the students to discuss, struggle, and learn for themselves by trial and error. A trained teacher can explain how to operate a tape-recorder much more efficiently than if a class tried to resolve the procedure for themselves. Thanks to lectures, too, Confucius' wisdom was brought to many minds instead of each student labor-iously drawing the same conclusions on his own.

No other method can transmit so much to so many with such effectiveness as the lecture. This method, when em-ployed by a competent teacher, can also make a complex or involved procedure much clearer to the student than a book can, especially because the observant lecturer knows when an additional illustration is necessary.

The lecture can provide exposure to material not found in the readings but considered essential by the instructor and, of course, this factual matter gains vividness in the person of a skillful lecturer. Sparkling eyes, a tilt of the head, a wave of the hand, the formation of a sudden dimple and many other gestures can be meaningful in heightening the warm proceedings and person-to-person communication of a lecture, in contrast to the dull and drab black-on-white of the textbook.

Although criticized forcefully and frequently, the lecture remains a strong, versatile, and functional method when properly used. Effective utilization is naturally the key to the lecture method's success—as it is with all methods of teaching.

Certain limitations of this method cannot be overlooked in our evaluation of the lecture. Aside from the fact that the lecture method places at a serious disadvantage those students who have not learned to take notes, this method of teaching tends to be a one-way process which places the student in a passive role. There is also the danger that the teacher may only be restating or repeating what a pupil could easily understand by a quick reading of a few paragraphs in a textbook. Furthermore, it is difficult for a teacher to determine immediately whether or not the students are learning and, of course, there is the possibility that the teacher himself may be poorly equipped, either by temperament or inclination, to lecture well.

Despite its disadvantages, the lecture does, however, provide a unique organizing or integrating feature in the presentation of learning material. In fact, we might compare the lecture to the human body. Just as the body is flexible —we are able to stretch, move, and position ourselves for certain tasks and activities—so can our minds be enlightened, molded, and changed by explanation and teaching.

A book, on the other hand, is like a block of wood; once the words have been run off the press, nothing can be changed. The author of a book only has one chance to strike a hit. The lecturer, however, goes to bat day after day.

4. THE SOCRATIC METHOD

Can you substantiate your claim?

The exhortation "Know thyself" has long been a clue to successful individual development. Once a student can recognize his weaknesses and limitations as well as his talents and attributes, he is well on his way toward the attainment of true learning.

The first great teacher to stress this importance of self-knowledge was Socrates (?470-399 B.C.), whose philosophy rested on a firm belief in the absolute reality and necessity of virtue. He maintained that the one true way to virtue was by knowledge, and knowledge of human things and especially of ourselves is the first essential of wisdom and goodness alike.

Socrates' method of teaching developed as a direct consequence of some extreme abuses of the lecture method by a group known as the Sophists who were instructing the Athenian youth at that time. These Sophists exultantly claimed that they possessed knowledge of all things and, in turn, were paid well by the Greek parents for communicating this knowledge to their children. Lecturing to little groups of students usually gathered in a private home or *stoa* (a portico used as an assembly area), the Sophists taught grammar, rhetoric, dialectic, and mathematics. Many of them, however, were more intent on displaying their wisdom than imparting the truth.

Socrates was also a brilliant teacher. In contrast to the Sophists, however, he never claimed to possess wisdom but instead asserted that he loved it. A true lover (*philos*) of wisdom (*sophia*), or "philosopher," Socrates openly declared a yearning to learn instead of pretending to know all things.

Although he did not conduct a school in the formal sense, Socrates did reach many pupils. He would walk the streets of Athens talking with the youth or even with the Sophists themselves, in efforts to develop clear ideas about virtue.

While the wind softly swept through the olive branches surrounding the Erechtheum of the Acropolis, Socrates would sit his students down on the grass near the broad Ionic columns of the temple. As soon as he had engaged a young man in conversation, Socrates would always admit his own ignorance first and assert that others were wiser than he. He would then ask not for examples but definitions of such virtues as courage, temperance, justice, or beauty. Then by clever and calculated questioning, Socrates would lead his students to a series of important concessions. Besides acknowledging that he really did not know the essential meaning of the term he had used, the student also was led to recognize that his own ideas were confused and some of his statements self-contradictory.

Such is the dialog as Socrates challenges his student Agathon.

> "*I think you said something like this; the gods arranged their business through love of beautiful things, for there could not be a love for ugly things. Didn't you say something like that?*"
>
> "*Yes, I did,*" said Agathon.
>
> "*And quite reasonably too, my friend,*" said Socrates; "*and if this is so, would not Love be love of beauty, not of ugliness?*"

> *He agreed.*
> *"Well now, it has been agreed that he loves what he lacks and has not?"*
> *"Yes," Agathon said.*
> *"Then Love lacks and has not beauty."*
> *"That must be," said he.*
> *"Very well; do you say that what lacks beauty and in no wise has beauty is beautiful?"*
> *"Certainly not."*
> *"Then if that is so, do you still agree that Love is beautiful? . . . Can you substantiate your claim?"*
> *Agathon answered, "I fear, Socrates, I knew nothing of what I said!"*[1]

Thus Agathon fell victim to the "Socratic irony." In other words, he realized that what he had said was as incongruous with the truth as Christmas in July, and he was consequently forced to admit that he did not know what he was talking about. In this manner, Socrates flattened or "ironed" out his opponents and made them concede that they lacked knowledge. So profound was the effect of this system that it changed the meaning of the word "irony," which had originally meant "interrogation" in Greek.

Socrates was not one to leave his opponents or students devastated after their admission of ignorance. The learner was now receptive for a new series of questions which Socrates would carefully plan. As a result, the individual would not only fully comprehend the narrowness of his original concept, but he would also conceive new ideas and conclusions after this extensive and intensive search of his mind.

This lasting sense of self-discovery achieved by the student was the goal toward which the Socratic method was geared, and, as employed by this Greek sage, it was indeed

[1] Plato, "Symposium," in *Great Dialogues of Plato*, translated by W. H. D. Rouse (New York: The New American Library of World Literature, Inc., 1956), pp. 96-97.

successful in bringing men to essential knowledge and skills through basic principles.

The Socratic method, as originated by the fifth-century B.C master himself, enjoys the same basic characteristics today. Conversational in structure, the method is two-fold in nature:

1. *Ironic.* This is the negative stage during which Socrates or the modern-day teacher tests the student by successive questions on a certain concept to reveal the learner's ignorance. Just as Socrates endeavored to dispel the erroneous positions of his Sophist colleagues on beauty or goodness, so the twentieth-century educator might demonstrate a student's misinterpretation of a certain geometric theorem by leading him to discover its inadequacy in solving a particular problem. Called Socratic irony to this day, this step is necessary in the quest for knowledge, for no one can learn until he becomes humble and acknowledges his present lack of wisdom.

2. *Maieutic.* Once the student is provoked by the teacher's questioning to admit his own ignorance, this positive, or maieutic, phase of the Socratic method begins. Although similar to the ironic aspect, in that information is elicited from the student by questions, this second series of questions is distinguished by a calculated attempt on the part of the teacher to link empirical observations by mental organization and then to lead the student to arrive at universal concepts with true understanding.

While the mental work in such a process is obviously done in great part by the questioner, the student is given the opportunity to view the end result as his very own reasoning and conclusion. In this sense, Socrates claimed that he was acting as an intellectual midwife (*maia*) because he was merely assisting at the birth of ideas in the minds of his students. The twentieth-century teacher might play this role as he guides a student who knows that one angle in an equilateral triangle equals 60° to discover that each angle in all triangles of this type must equal 60°.

Essentially, the Socratic method is heuristic, that is, a method by which the student finds out a solution for himself by examination. The mental process by which the student uses this heuristic method to reach new knowledge is call induction.

The *inductive technique* requires the student to proceed from the particular to the general, to draw a definition from the logical grouping of many related but separate sense impressions. These definitions, being formed as universals, establish a firm and lasting foundation for human knowledge.

Viewing the definitions that the Sophists presented in their lectures as inadequate, Socrates further maintained that their tailormade answers were a hindrance to proper reasoning. Often when these men, who claimed to know everything, were engaged in discourse on a lofty subject, Socrates would quietly interrupt to ask them, *"To-Ti?"* (What is it?) to which no satisfactory answer could be found.

SUMMARY

Socrates himself suggested that psychological, ethical, and religious truths were the best areas for the utilization of his method. The search for truths of this nature could be pursued either by the intuitions of reason and common sense or by a natural induction.

To be sure, the Socratic method would prove most frustrating to teacher and pupil alike if it were attempted in courses of study concerned primarily with the dissemination of facts, such as history, geography, geology, and astronomy. It would indeed be very difficult, if not impossible, for a student to know that the Declaration of Independence was

signed in 1776 by a purely inductive process of learning.
It should also be stressed that the Socratic method is
most suitable for use on the collegiate or graduate level,
particularly in programs where general principles are being
sought, such as philosophy, theology, and some advanced
education courses. In order to obtain significant results
from this method the students should possess some background on the topic to be developed.

Those who wish to use this Socratic method should be
further advised to practice the various phases with extreme
care. A teacher must never use the negative phase of questioning to badger or bewilder an honest and docile student.
Indeed the teacher must be quite discriminating as to "his
victim" in order to avoid the slightest risk of psychological
harm to a learner. It must always be remembered that after
"flattening" the person with Socratic irony, the teacher must
then work even harder to build up the student's understanding and ability to discover true meanings.

Still another limitation of this method is the imposing
requirement of time and patience which it demands of the
teacher in order to be effective. The teacher must also realize that he has to be willing to allow the student to make
errors in his answers before guiding him to proper conclusions. Too often when a teacher has a right answer, the
temptation becomes very great to deliver it to the student
directly by a lecture. It is far more meaningful for the student, however, to question and discover for himself in this
time-consuming process of education.

Of course it takes a particularly skillful teacher with a
thorough mastery of the subject matter to develop facility
with such a rapid-fire yet logical system of questioning.
Once this is accomplished, however, the Socratic method's
advantage of stimulated interest and the animated give and
take between teacher and student are apparent.

Not only is it a unique and heartening delight for a
teacher to witness the gains of his pupils through the judi-

cious use of this method, but real thought on the part of the learner is certainly assured. There is the additional guarantee of life being breathed into an otherwise uninspiring topic when a student can claim, "Now I see. . . . No one told me. . . . I discovered it for myself!"

As the pioneer in such a rational approach to teaching, Socrates bequeathed a significant legacy to the pursuit of wisdom. By maintaining that learning is not so much a process of gathering information as it is seeing meanings, this great teacher helped his students to "know themselves" so that they might recognize their ignorance, remedy it, and ultimately achieve wisdom and virtue.

How effectively a teacher applies the Socratic method today depends to a large extent on how closely he matches the characteristics of the method's original exponent. The tact, wisdom, humility, and eloquence of a Socrates are attributes not easily attained.

5. THE DISCUSSION METHOD

Let's analyze what has been said thus far. . . .

How many times have we passed a few ladies animatedly discussing the latest dress styles? How often have we also watched a group of men analyzing the latest news about the stock market and voicing their views on its trends?

Although we may chuckle and conclude that the gentlemen are trying to determine how they will stretch their dollars to pay for the ladies' new fashions, we cannot help but realize that such interaction of opinions frequently produces new insights and conclusions about the topic at hand.

While it is most probable that people have been discussing problems since they first began to speak, it is on the Roman civilization that we focus to see some of the most persuasive uses of discussion as a form of instruction. Here we look to the Roman Forum, not a classroom, and to the great orator Cicero, not a formal teacher, for another major contribution to educational theory prior to the dawning of the Christian era.

Marcus Tullius Cicero (106-43 B.C.) was a leading statesman whose many orations, such as *De Amicitia* and *De Senectute,* are even now praised for their excellence of style and thought. He believed most strongly that to be an ideal citizen one must be adept at oratory.

Before the dynamic strains of his famous Senate addresses resounded throughout the Capitoline Hill, Cicero often engaged his colleagues in a discussion on the topic under consideration. He would first carefully elicit differing opinions while simultaneously attempting to narrate and guide the dialog. Cicero would then endeavor to formulate general conclusions of true value.

In fact it would not be unrealistic to imagine Cicero stimulating a discussion in the following fashion:

> *"My fellow senators, as members of this august body, it is our responsibilty to formulate the best policies to preserve the grandeur and glory of the Roman empire. To this end, let us now discuss 'How we may best educate our citizens.' Tell us, Catiline, what is your opinion?"*
>
> *"Truly the bravery of our warriors has brought us world conquest,"* Catiline would reply, *"but the great Roman wall which I have seen extend through miles of English countryside must yet encompass the world. It is, therefore, with military prowess that we should train our citizens."*
>
> *"I see,"* said Cicero, *"for you, the good citizen must be trained in the bravery of battle. Does everyone agree?"*
>
> *"Nay, it is the aesthete who will make the best citizen for Rome!"* interjected Caelius. *"My slave is Greek and he has taught me much about the beauties of life. Indeed I say it is only when we can appreciate beauty like the Greeks that we will have the best civilization in the world."*
>
> *"Aesthetic appreciation to develop the whole man is your goal, Caelius, and a worthy viewpoint too, as is Catiline's. It seems that Catiline's aim is akin to that of the Spartans while Caelius wants us to be like the Athenians. Does anyone else have a different idea?"*
>
> *"I do, Cicero, but I do not look to any of the Greeks, but to the Hebrews instead,"* said Esquilus. *"They worship Yahweh and I have seen that their citizens are loyal and their life in Palestine is a good one. We must*

therefore look to our gods, Lares and Penates, and place our trust in them. If we respect the gods, then we will develop the best citizens for Rome."

"Belief in the gods will provide the best citizens according to Esquilus," said Cicero as he began to summarize. "My fellow senators, we have heard three very different opinions from which we must choose a solution to our problem of how to best educate our citizens. . . . Let us first analyze what has been said thus far.

"Do we need the quality of courage, an aesthetic appreciation for beauty, or devotion to the gods? Indeed I believe we need all three! To these we must also add the forcefulness and logic of an orator to achieve the greatest good.

"An orator," concluded Cicero, "is an ideally educated citizen—he must be brave in all encounters, he must praise the finest attributes of his nation, and he must engender loyalty to the gods who guide the land. One must be able to speak in the Forum with wisdom so that the Magnum Imperium may achieve the Pax Romana forever. To be a good citizen, one must first be trained as a good orator."

From this illustration we can see how Cicero might have used the varying opinions of his fellow men to derive foundations for the particular viewpoint he wished to present. In this instance, Cicero wanted to help others to learn the importance of oratory. By linking the abilities others deemed important for a good citizen to the qualities of a good orator, Cicero led the others to concude with him that "a good citizen must first be a good orator."

It becomes evident that the discussion method of teaching is a "hybrid" embracing various characteristics of the memorization, Socratic, and lecture methods. Just as some background knowledge, easily gained by memorization, is essential to an intelligent discussion, we also find a series of lecture-type statements and Socratic questions, although these declarations and queries originate from all parts of the room.

While diversified in composition, the discussion method is basically defined as a supervised conversation during which the students take an active role by stating their views on a certain topic, at the same time that the teacher guides the group to discern certain unifying principles.

Although the discussion method is one of the most popular techniques in use today, it is important to note that only in the modern times of democratic classroom procedures has it gained such prominence. Strict discipline, a formal approach, and a "the child should be seen and not heard" attitude are clearly incompatible with this method of teaching.

Consequently, to be most effective, the discussion method should be used only in areas where the course, to some extent at least, is aimed at developing ideals and instilling habits of thinking and investigating.

It is most essential, too, that the students have substantial familiarity with a topic before it can be discussed. The memorization of a poem or a set of principles might even be required beforehand. When such material is eventually discussed, everyone is acquainted with the basic content, although each may interpret it variously. A teacher must remember also that facts, as such, cannot be discussed; for example, it would be futile to hear various opinions on the fact that $2 + 2 = 4$.

The actual practice of the discussion method embraces three broad stages:

1. *Presentation* is the introduction of the problem or topic to the students for their opinions, evaluations, or solutions. It is crucial that the teacher be aware of his specific aim for the lesson from the very beginning and, tactfully, lead the students toward achieving that learning goal through their own discussion. Cicero fully intended to praise the merits of oratory for Roman citizens before he led his

colleagues in discussion on the preparation of a good citizen.

2. *Guidance* is the continual and purposeful direction which the teacher gives the students throughout the discussion. This interaction and exchange of comments on the teacher's part helps to clarify and unite the opinions that are offered in relation to the overall aim of the lesson. This also insures that all will have an equal opportunity to contribute and that no one individual will dominate the group. Cicero made sure that each man was heard and commented himself as the discussion progressed.

3. *Summary* is the recapitulation of important points revealed in the course of the discussion. Although these resolutions, judgments, or clarifications are generally summarized by the teacher, often a student may be selected to conclude a particular discussion in this manner. Cicero acted like many teachers in summarizing the qualities of a good citizen in our imaginary discussion, but he could have asked a participant to give the summary.

During all three stages of the discussion, the teacher should strive to promote a natural, tensionless atmosphere, while remaining in control. Just as the toga-clad senators were not suppressed in their views, today's students should not be stifled by feeling that they are being quizzed or rated on their opinions.

Verbal skills, consequently, should be cultivated by this emphasis on oral expression and participation, although accurate thinking is the primary requirement. The teacher should likewise be alert and adept at recasting a student's phraseology so that everyone may understand a certain opinion as it is asserted.

The successful practice of the discussion method also requires an important combination of special C's on the part of the students—*comprehension*, *confidence*, and *courtesy*.

The first of these, *comprehension*, demands real thought

and reflection from the pupils. They must draw on past learnings and use their reasoning powers to substantiate meaningful and logical opinions.

Confidence helps the students to feel reassured of their ability to communicate ideas. The students should be relaxed and comfortable so that they will not hesitate to participate in the discussion.

Courtesy means respect for the opinions of others. Willingness to give everyone a fair hearing is crucial to an orderly and successful discussion. Students must be patient with each other, just as the teacher must be extremely tolerant and display equanimity of expression throughout an entire lesson of this nature.

One further guideline for teachers is that, when employing the discussion method, there is no *one* right answer even if there is only one aim.

In a social studies lesson on railroads, students might be asked to discuss "What country has the best railroads—the United States, Canada, or Japan?" One student might very well say that Japan's are best because they can travel the fastest at 300 m.p.h., but still other students might favor the American or Canadian railroads for reasons of safety and comfort. In the course of the discussion, many new facts concerning railroad travel will be learned by the group, although personal preference will dictate which is best for an individual traveler.

A primary level teacher can likewise stimulate a discussion when he says "Let's talk about . . ." One such topic might be "The Vegetables That Grow in the Garden." One youngster might like corn and want to describe it, whereas another child may prefer spinach or squash.[1] While many preferences might be cited throughout the lesson, the important thing is that many new facts about the size, shape,

---

[1] The fundamental proverb *De gustibus non est disputandum* (Concerning tastes there should be no disputing) should naturally prevail in this setting as in all discussions.

color, and taste of these vegetables will be shared by the students.

Although all the children probably will not agree on which vegetable tastes best, the teacher will have an opportunity to impart some general facts about science, health, and social studies. Such a lesson might also enable the teacher to interject some spelling facts to reenforce learning. It may be true that all children may not share the same opinion about corn, spinach, or squash, but they will have to agree that there is only one correct way to spell each of these words.

Perhaps the discussion method displays its greatest utility on the collegiate and graduate levels. Hypothetical situations encompassing practical problems in education may be explored in depth. In the process of discussing these problems, students can advance tentative hypotheses as possible solutions. They can also exchange views with others. This provides the possibility of encountering strong disagreement which might be a very healthy thing at this stage of their education.

SUMMARY

More than any other method explored thus far, the discussion is particularly valuable because it offers social growth as well as individual development. Not only is each student encouraged in habits of clear thinking, but an appreciation of the common goals of the group is also instilled in the entire class. Just as each learner is taught to make generalizations and draw conclusions, so also the whole class becomes aware of the importance of shared responsibility in contributing to group solidarity. The social aims of interrelation and mutual understanding consequently are fostered at all times throughout a discussion lesson.

The advantages of the discussion method are many. By

interaction and oral expression, the student is obliged to take a vital role in the learning process and this is usually accompanied by that ever-desirable activity—thinking.

Furthermore, since only topics with which the students can claim basic familiarity should be discussed, interest is usually maintained by this steady flow of thought and the expression of various points of view. Students are also freed from being forced to accept the dogmatic assertions of a teacher by working out their particular difficulties through discussion. In the relaxed and tensionless atmosphere of a discussion, a learner usually feels much easier about calling upon the teacher for the clarification of obscure points or even the repetition of forgotten facts.

This method of teaching also draws the teacher and students into close harmony as coworkers on a common problem. In so doing, the rate of teaching equals or corresponds to the rate of learning because all must proceed toward the particular learning goal as a group, hearing and evaluating individual opinions together.

Obviously, however, certain limitations are inherent in the very nature of a discussion lesson. Topics about which the pupils have little or no facts would lead to irrelevant discussion and little learning. Loquacious students or truly brilliant scholars often attempt to monopolize the conversation to a tedious degree if a teacher is not a skillful leader.

There is also the danger that the informal atmosphere, conducive to good discussions, may be used by some students in an attempt to disrupt the class. These unruly students may try to take advantage of the method to forget discipline altogether. A teacher must also make certain that a majority opinion does not run roughshod or rule out the small group with another solution to the problem being discussed. Another crucial consideration in evaluating the effectiveness of the discussion method is the individual teacher's ability to guide the class in its discussion while preserving the atmosphere of a group project.

Although deemed by many as the panacea or cure-all in educational methodology, the discussion method—like all methods of teaching—is not sufficient in itself. The discussion requires not only proper material and the right time for its use, but particularly the judgment of a skillful leader to achieve the most constructive and meaningful learning.

6. THE PARABLE METHOD

And He spoke to them in parables . . .

Teaching is like gardening. If a gardener wishes to grow a rosebush, he must first select the correct time of year, plant a shoot, and then cultivate the soil around it. If the gardener has prepared the soil properly, nature will soon take its course and stems will take root and eventually buds will spring forth.

But this is not all. Teaching is also like gardening because the gardener must break off bad leaves, pull out weeds, and watch out for thorns. After this exacting preparation, the gardener can now present to the mistress of the manor a particular rose which he has assisted God in producing.

We could also compare the teacher to a mother nourishing her young, to a sculptor forming a monument, or to any other craftsman whose artistry helps to actualize the potential of an object entrusted to his care.

To compare teaching to other arts in this manner is a kind of parable. Although history records that parables were used frequently by King Solomon and Socrates had used parables as well, it is customary to associate this method of teaching with the Master, Jesus Christ.

As the Greatest Teacher of all time, Our Lord explained the important truths of mankind's salvation and illustrated His teaching by means of parables. On the hillside, in the

temple, at the marriage feast, in the garden, on the roadside
—everywhere He went—Christ taught the people to seek the
things that are above and not the things that are on the
earth. He prepared His listeners for the truths of His message by presenting analogies of familiar objects as compared
to the sublime reality of life everlasting: The kingdom of
heaven is like "a grain of mustard seed" or "a wedding
feast" or "a pearl of great price."

By using forms of speech and illustrations related to the
previous knowledge of the people, Christ placed the point
of His parables easily within their comprehension. Consequently, a farmer could not soon forget the parable of the
sower, nor could the Pharisees overlook that of the husband-
man and his wicked servants.

Let us pause a moment and observe three of the greatest
lessons ever presented:

> The kingdom of heaven is like a grain of mustard seed,
> which a man took and sowed in his field.
> This is indeed the smallest of all the seeds; but when it
> grows up it is larger than any herb and becomes a tree, so
> that the birds of the air come and dwell in its branches.[1]
>
> The kingdom of heaven is like a treasure hidden in a
> field; he who finds it hides it, and in his joy goes and
> sells all that he has and buys that field.
> Again, the kingdom of heaven is like a merchant in
> search of fine pearls.
> When he finds a single pearl of great price, he goes and
> sells all that he has and buys it.[2]
>
> Again, the kingdom of heaven is like a net cast into the
> sea that gathered in fish of every kind.
> When it was filled, they hauled it out, and sitting down
> on the beach, they gathered the good fish into vessels,
> but threw away the bad.
> So will it be at the end of the world. The angels will go

[1] Matthew 13:31-32.
[2] Matthew 13:44-46.

out and separate the wicked from among the just; and will cast them into the furnace of fire, where there will be the weeping, and the gnashing of teeth.[3]

On still other occasions, Our Lord referred to the seed, the cockle, the fig tree, to the wind and the rain, to vines and vineyards, to sheep and the shepherd, to farmers and fishermen, to the hen and her chicks, to the birds of the air, and to the lilies of the field—indeed to most of the sights and sounds and scenes familiar to the people.

Hence the ordinary experiences of daily life were woven into the parables of the sower, the vineyard workers, the wedding guests, and many more. In all of these comparison stories, Jesus not only captured the imagination, but most effectively taught the people His doctrine.

In delivering these parables, Our Lord combined lecture, discussion, and questioning techniques. He served as a Living Model for His teachings and by His example truly taught all men how to live. In giving example as well as precept, Our Lord invited all men of all ages to imitate Him, to "teach all nations."[4] Certainly the parable method is as advantageous now as it was when it was used by the Divine Teacher.

Everyone, young and old alike, loves a story, and a parable is precisely that. Although some may claim this method of teaching cannot be as effective in our sophisticated society as it was in the simpler times of Christ, this assertion is difficult to justify. Whether the comparison is detailed or concise, the parable remains a particularly appealing teaching device.

The word parable is derived from the Greek word *parabole,* meaning "to throw" or "put by the side of," hence, "to compare," and can be defined as a simple narra-

---

[3] Matthew 13:47-50.
[4] Matthew 28:19.

tive in which the abstract is explained by the familiar in order to present certain moral or theoretical truths and principles.

Just as we previously compared teaching to gardening, so also can a teacher prepare the student's mind to grasp unfamiliar concepts by drawing an analogy to familiar knowledge.

Of its nature, the parable method is less formal than the discussion, Socratic, or lecture methods. For this reason, it is extremely flexible and useful from kindergarten through college. In fact, the parable is not only versatile as a method of teaching, but it is also an excellent means to stimulate interest and motivate a lesson.

Essentially, the parable proceeds in the following manner:

1. *Statement of analogy.* In this initial step, the teacher presents a certain analogy or declares with what familiar concept something less well known can be compared. "The kingdom of heaven is like a mustard seed," Christ said; modern teachers could easily say, "Teaching is like gardening."

2. *Description of detail.* The teacher next reveals many of the characteristics of the familiar analog. Just as Christ pointed to the properties of the mustard seed (its minuteness and the fact that it grows into a large tree), so also are the details of gardening (the clipping of the decaying leaves, the uprooting of the nearby weeds) necessary for the audience to appreciate the teacher's message. In detail, discussion on the right time for planting could show that a student must be ready for a certain concept; cultivation of the soil could illustrate the student's need for the necessary instruction and enrichment, just as letting nature take its course could remind us that the student must not be pressed beyond his ability. In plucking weeds and unhealthy leaves, we see that the student must be protected from bad influences, and, in overcoming thorns, he must pass cer-

tain tests. Only after all of this preparation does the garden flower or can the student be accepted at the highest level for graduation. In this way, the unknown is not defined as a term directly, but is compared to a like concept, with similar characteristics which are familiar to the learner.

3. *Conclusions* must finally be drawn as the analogy is brought to a close. If the student does not immediately understand the parallel, then often a teacher might be required to point out the comparisons more explicitly. Once the student grasps the point of the analogy, then new learning has been achieved.

Throughout the entire presentation, the pupil is challenged directly or by implication to apply the analogy to the new subject matter at hand. In fact, as soon as the teacher presents the initial statement of comparison, a question should form in the student's mind: "How is this less-known thing like something previously known?" or, "How is teaching like gardening?"

As he follows the extended metaphor during the presentation, the student is continually asking himself that question. The aim of the teacher in delivering the parable is to bring the pupil to pass an affirmative judgment on the validity of the comparison at the end of the lesson. Thus the student becomes involved in the development of the parable as he *questions himself* and *seeks to form a judgment*. Such a subtle notion of mystery or discovery helps to sustain a high degree of interest in the parable. As the student grows more involved in seeking to answer his own question, he becomes more and more eager to hear the metaphor fully extended and to resolve the question in his mind.

Since the student is proceeding from the realm of known material in search of an unknown concept, the illustration or composition of the parable must be vivid and understandable. The images must be clear and concrete, although the exact relationship remains somewhat of a mystery until the analogy is complete. It is for this reason that the teacher must endeavor to keep the subject of comparison before the student's mind. Although details must be revealed and concepts related, throughout the parable the teacher must carefully and continually reiterate the main idea to the students (teaching is like gardening) so they will not become absorbed in technicalities and miss the point.

Naturally, the success of the parable depends to a great extent on the ability of the teacher to tell a story. Not only should the teacher be proficient in relating the details of the parable, but he must also be careful not to give away the ending before he has drawn a complete analogy. Much thoughtful preparation is consequently a crucial prerequisite to the delivery of a good parable. Not only must details be gathered and relationships perceived, but they must also be planned for presentation in simple, clear, and meaningful terms. If for some reason the analogy is later found to be weak or unclear at a certain point, then a teacher must likewise be patient and willing to explain and elucidate the details still further.

As mentioned before, the parable method's effectiveness easily spans a kindergarten-to-college range. The most important consideration in adopting it for the various levels is naturally the degree of suitability of the particular subject matter to be analogized. It is generally agreed that nature study, literature, history, morals, and religion best lend themselves to this technique.

A lesson on courage would probably not be too meaningful if the virtue were explained merely by means of a dictionary definition. A parable about Joan of Arc, however, which compares her heroic actions of fortitude and bravery in defense of her faith and country—even at the threat of being burned at the stake—surely would help students to understand what courage is like.

SUMMARY

The teacher of today should not overlook the excellent pedagogical technique of the parable, which enables a student to comprehend abstract truths and intricate concepts by comparison with familiar knowledge. No other method achieves clarity with such precision.

Because of its storylike format, the parable almost automatically guarantees a student's attention. Unlike fables, which deal with unreal situations like talking animals, parables deal with authentic and lifelike comparisons. The parable also draws the student into self-activity as he seeks to absorb the analogy by continual self-questioning (*Why* is teaching like gardening?).

The teacher must be careful to stress emphatically the point of comparison, however, because experience shows that a pupil often remembers the story but fails to remember the principle for which the analogy was made. Even though the story provides enjoyment and entertainment for the student, the teacher should not make the story an end in itself.

The parable is a *means* to new learning. In telling the story of Joan of Arc, it is true that the class does become fascinated by the narrative but, most importantly, the virtue of courage will be appreciated and understood in the process.

Essentially the parable is not meant so much to startle as it is to persuade. Indeed, a good parable not only wins, but it convinces as well.

7. THE SCHOLASTIC METHOD

On the contrary, it seems that . . .

When Jesus Christ established His Church on earth, He commissioned His apostles and their successors "to go forth and teach all nations" (Matthew 28:19). For the first few hundred years that followed its establishment, the Church of Christ was beset by many persecutions. Consequently, the early fathers were often forced to seek refuge underground. These tunnels and passageways below the surface of the earth in Rome and elsewhere were known as catacombs.

It was in these catacombs that instruction in the Christian faith was frequently given and many converts won. Before a candidate was allowed to enter into a catacomb, however, certain passwords or secret signals had to be given, for fear that a traitor might expose the faithful Christians to the rapacity of the Roman emperor and his cohorts.

Once granted admittance into the catacomb, the candidate was carefully taught the truths revealed by Christ. The method that the early Christians used was characterized by the rigid memorization of a particular set of questions, followed by certain equally rigid answers. Termed the "catechetical method" from the Greek word *catechesis,* this means of instruction permitted no freedom on the part of the individual (the catechumen) to deviate from the prescribed answers which the teacher (the catechist) had presented. It was the catechist's responsibility to ascertain the orthodoxy of the catechumen's belief and, once this was done, the candidate was admitted to the most sacred part of the liturgy. In essence the catechetical method of instruction may be equated with the memorization procedure already considered; consequently, it will not be reviewed here.

The issuance of the Edict of Milan by Constantine in 313 brought Christianity into the daylight, however, and the Church began to flourish and grow. At that time, although there were no schools as we know them, centers of learning were established and maintained in the monasteries of the Benedictines and other religious communities. ·

Otherwise known as the Dark Ages, this period looked to the monks and such scholars as Saints Augustine, Basil the Great, and John Chrysostom, and to Boethius and Tertullian to preserve the knowledge of mankind.

The Western world was simultaneously experiencing driving invasions by such pagan tribes as the Huns, Goths, and Visigoths. As the continent of Europe was overrun, it also became the task of the Church to convert these pagans. Saints Boniface, Cyril, Methodius, and Patrick were among those sent out to teach the fundamentals of Christianity to the barbarians.

St. Patrick has been particularly revered through the centuries for bringing the Faith to Ireland. Millions have heard the story of St. Patrick's explaining the mystery of the Trinity by holding up a three-leafed shamrock. This famed lesson was not only an early example of using concrete objects to teach abstract ideas, but, by tradition, it has also given Ireland a national emblem. It is also a fact of history that, in the centuries following St. Patrick's death, so many monastic schools were established in Ireland that the country became known as "the Isle of Saints and Scholars" and students flocked to it from all over Europe.

As preachers, St. Patrick and these other leaders of the Church did much to teach the principles of life and learning, but it was not until the establishment of the Holy Roman Empire by Charlemagne in the year 800 that formal schooling became a concern. During the reign of Charlemagne, Alcuin, the equivalent of a modern lord chancellor of education, initiated a system of palace schools to train the youth. Besides religious instruction, the curriculum emphasized reading and writing, as well as the *trivium* (grammar, logic, and rhetoric) and the *quadrivium* (arithmetic, music, geometry, and astronomy).

During this period, a system of cathedral schools also began to flourish. These schools took their name from the fact that they were frequently conducted in the main church of a diocese, the cathedral, which is so named because it is the place where the bishop has his main seat or *cathedra*. Although frequently maintained to train young men for the priesthood, these cathedral schools also played a large part in the acceptance and development of a general schooling procedure.

In fact from these rudimentary beginnings emerged the organization of several universities by the year 1200. The people at these universities, known as Scholastics (or people of the schools) gathered as a body of masters and students in pursuit of the intellectual life on the highest level of specialization.

Paris, Padua, Bologna, and Salerno were among the centers of learning which received their charters from the Pope or emperor during this time. Because these universities provided scholarly opportunities, their charters granted them special privileges. Exemption from taxation and military service as well as immunity of person and special courts outside civil jurisdiction were guaranteed to the university community. The Scholastics were also accorded the power to grant licenses to teach and the privilege known as *cessatio*, or suspending work as a protest against local persecutions.

These universities were composed essentially of teachers and students; there were no campuses or large physical structures such as we consider so necessary today. Class would meet wherever a particular master decided, with the students following the teacher of their choice and remaining with him as he gave instruction. The teacher spoke from a raised platform, and the pupils usually sat on benches copying notes. Often, if a particularly large group wished to hear a certain master, and no other accommodations were adequate, or if the weather was inclement, a cathedral would become a classroom.

The instruction given in these medieval universities was frequently in the form of a commentary given by the teacher as he read the text of a noted author. Basically this method of teaching is the same as the lecture technique and will not be repeated here. In addition, the professor often employed the disputation as an educational device. The disputation consisted of four definite phases. (1) A thesis would be proposed by a particular student; (2) proof supporting the thesis would be offered; (3) objections would be raised by the teacher or fellow students and as a result, (4) the thesis would be accepted or rejected.

The Scholastics used this formal and rigorous approach to learning in many of their philosophical discussions. A student also had to stand for an extraordinary disputation in order to receive his culminating degree from the university. It was at the extraordinary disputation that a particular candidate had to establish the validity of his thesis to the satisfaction of the entire university community.

However, this period should also be remembered for the introduction of the method of the *Summa*. Commonly known as the *Scholastic Method*, this procedure was masterfully used by Thomas Aquinas. As illustrated in his scholarly compendium the *Summa Theologica*, and in his other profound works, St. Thomas' teachings have more deeply influenced learning than any other collection of the Scholastic age.

During the years 1256 to 1259, the lessons of St. Thomas were delivered in Latin to the students of the University of Paris gathered around him. Thomas would start by asking his students a question of a theological or philosophical nature, such as "Does God exist or not?" or "Does the human mind receive knowledge from sensible things?"

Let us imagine, for example, the scene when the students were presented with the question, "Can one man teach another?" While they began to think about teaching and the attributes of a teacher, St. Thomas outlined a series of the most cogent and authoritatively supported objections which seemed to deny the assertion involved in his initial question.

Just as his students were about to conclude that "it appears one man cannot teach another," St. Thomas cited a source which alleged the truth of the opposing view, "But the contrary is what the Apostle says (I Timothy 2:7), 'Of that witness I am the chosen herald, sent as an apostle . . . to be a true and faithful teacher of the Gentiles'" (*Summa Theologica*, I, q. 117, a. 1).

Next St. Thomas proceeded to elaborate on all of the reasons why this contrary position must be the true solution to the question. He not only proved that "the master leads the disciple from things known to knowledge of the unknown," but also gave valid references to substantiate his explanation.

In conclusion, St. Thomas finished his lesson by answering all the objections presented earlier which had seemed to support the negative view. Thus, in a most convincing and definitely logical manner, St. Thomas would not only teach his students basic truths and their proofs, but he would also prepare them to overcome some of the most challenging objections they might encounter. Because St. Thomas recorded his lessons in the *Summa* and other compendiums, the learners of the present century can benefit just as did the Scholastics who faithfully followed this great teacher day after day in the medieval university.

The twentieth-century teacher might expand Aquinas' question and wonder, "Can one man teach another . . . with the Scholastic method today?"

The scholastic method has five very definite phases:

1. *Quaestio*—the opening question posed by the teacher.
2. *Videtur*—presentation of the best objections that can be alleged for the negative answer to the question.
3. *E Contra*—assertion of the contrary to the above arguments.
4. *Respondeo*—the teacher's proof for the "e contra" opinion.
5. *Ad Primam*—point-by-point refutation of the objections raised earlier.

Perhaps the best way of proving that a modern lesson can be devised in the Scholastic framework would be to analyze the structure of the method by presenting a modern Scholastic's answer to the fundamental question.

(*Quaestio*) Can one man truly teach another?

(*Videtur*) Objection 1. It seems that one man cannot teach another because St. Augustine holds that the teacher is only giving signs to a pupil. Hence, no human being can teach any other human anything.

Objection 2. Further, Socrates says that a teacher is merely an intellectual midwife who assists a student in giving birth to his own idea.

(*E Contra*) On the contrary, St. Thomas holds that a teacher is someone who already possesses knowledge and reduces the potency in the student to act, and thus is someone who teaches another.

(*Respondeo*) I answer that St. Thomas actually holds

that there are only two modes of learning anything whatso-
ever. The first is by discovery without the aid of any other
human being, and the second is by instruction. A human
teacher influences a student as a secondary, not a principal,
cause of learning. It might even be better if we use the terms
"unaided" and "aided" to understand the two categories
of distinction.

Teachers are actually dispensable and totally unneces-
sary, according to St. Thomas, in the sense that teaching
must not be indoctrination, but rather the striving for an
active intellect on the part of the student. Still the teacher
functions as an auxiliary cause of learning. St. Thomas also
holds that the more instruction imitates that natural process
of discovery, the better it is.

To understand this most clearly, let us look at all the
arts. Art may be divided into four categories, the useful, the
fine, the liberal, and the basic or "cooperative" arts.

Of the basic arts, there are only three—farming, doctor-
ing, and teaching. The farmer cooperates with nature and
assists the vegetative soul in order that plants can grow. The
doctor cares for the animal soul and cooperates with nature
in the healing process. The teacher aids the rational soul
and helps the human being to perfect himself.

In the useful, fine, or liberal arts, an artist is one who
copies or *imitates the products of nature*, but, in the basic
or cooperative arts, the artist (farmer, doctor, or teacher) is
only an assistant who *imitates the way in which nature
operates*. For example, a physician, according to Hippocrates, has three ways of assisting his patient to recover, in
descending order: (1) a controlled regimen of his patient—a
good diet; (2) administration of drugs; and (3) surgery.

This is basically the same pattern a teacher employs:
(1) he may help the student by asking questions, assisting the
student in discovery; (2) he may teach by lecturing or tell-

ing, and (3) he may indoctrinate and expect verbal memory. St. Thomas maintained that learning the truth is the assimilation of the mind to reality. The most frequent mistake of a teacher is to think that learning is the assimilation of a student's mind to the teacher's mind. Instead we must realize that a good teacher steps aside and mediates the assimilation of a student's mind to reality.

As Mark Van Doren, the famous English literature scholar, once said in his lecture "The Teacher as a Person," the teacher is a person in the sense of the person of the drama. In the ancient Greek theater the actor held a mask before his face and made "sounds through" that mask. So also a teacher leads his pupils to the discovery of knowledge by the sounds he makes in his role as a teacher.

Wisdom is not conferred by the bestowal of a degree—it takes time. Since the teacher cannot make the pupil wise, perhaps it would be far more beneficial if we would merely teach the pupil how to learn.

(*Ad primam*) Reply to Objection 1: As St. Augustine says, when a teacher gives signs to the pupil, it is true that the pupil knew what these signs were about before. But this knowledge is present only in a general and confused way. A student did not appreciate the significance of the signs until the teacher pointed them out. In other words, the pupil did not possess perfect knowledge, but the teacher perfected him in knowledge.

Reply to Objection 2: In response to Socrates' view that a teacher is an intellectual midwife, I can answer that learning is not merely remembering. It cannot rightly be said that the human individual previously existed and his soul (now imprisoned in his body) is merely trying to recall what it knew in a previous existence. This is simply not the way in which learning takes place according to the famous principle of the Scholastics: *Nihil est in intellectu sine prior in sensibus* (Nothing is in the intellect without first being in the senses).

As shown in the above lesson on the function of a teacher, one can readily see that the formal structure of the Scholastic method of teaching can be tailored to accommodate the learners of the present century. A philosophy of education class could easily be the scene for the delivery of the preceding paragraphs.

Because of the rigid format of the Scholastic method, a teacher must be extremely well prepared in his presentation and the students must render careful attention to each step of the lesson. If the teacher should fail to substantiate one point, the entire validity of the argument might be destroyed. Naturally, also, the teacher must assimilate the material in terms which are on a level with the students' comprehension or the procedure will fail to prove anything to the learners.

It is obvious that this method of the *Summa* is an extremely profound method of argumentation. To explore questions in such depth, however, was quite common for the Scholastics. Today only those in very specialized fields of study would be able to make regular and profitable use of this method. Philosophy, theology, physics, astronomy, law, medicine, botany, and education are a few of the graduate or professional fields in which a teacher might introduce the Scholastic approach. In all such cases, both teacher and student alike would be expected to possess a fertile background of concepts and ideas from which the claims and reasoning might proceed.

SUMMARY

To achieve success in the use of St. Thomas' Scholastic method, a teacher must be willing to think and challenge his pupils to do likewise.

Not only must the teacher reason out all the ways to support the concept he wishes to teach, but he must also discover and solve all objections which can reasonably be raised. Furthermore, he must present these contrasting views thoroughly and fairly.

The Scholastic method, of course, requires a fantastic amount of preparation and research from the teacher for each individual lesson. This demands a great deal of time, and herein lies one of the serious limitations of this method in modern usage. Unless the hours of painstaking preparation are spent, however, there is the added risk that side issues or ramifications of a certain problem will go unexplored and the entire argument might consequently be proven invalid.

The many advantages of this method of the *Summa* make the tremendous effort one must expend worthwhile. The Scholastic method enables a teacher to render a truly complete presentation and thorough discussion of the given topic. No question goes unanswered in a student's mind. Since this method also sets forth arguments in a logical way, students are encouraged in independent habits of clear thinking and reasoning. The objections that the teacher raises are frequently far more astute than those students might have originated, and therefore their interest is sharpened as the lesson advances to each new stage of discovery.

Through Scholastic teaching, the student consequently learns in many ways—by questioning, listening, reasoning, and most of all by discovering. With St. Thomas Aquinas as a model, today's teacher can indeed bring learners to the affirmation of new truths with clarity and certainty. The guidance the teacher renders, however, must be marked by those same masterly qualities which the great Scholastics so finely embodied—wisdom, patience, and a very special dedication to the intellectual life.

8. THE JESUIT METHOD

The Ratio *is probably the most enduring of all educational regulations.* ULICH

In the long history of the world, many names and dates stand out in the progress of mankind. The arrival of Christopher Columbus on the American shores in 1492 is one such event which children quickly master as they begin their schooling. This consequently makes it very easy for students of the history of education to remember that the great teacher Juan Luis Vives (1492-1540), was born that same year in Valencia, Spain.

Although Vives, along with Erasmus and Budé, has long been regarded as a leader of the Humanists of the Northern Renaissance period in Europe, it is only recently that he has come to be recognized as a unique innovator and outstanding educator. Trained at the University of Paris, Vives later became a professor at the University of Louvain until his talents were discovered by Catherine of Aragon, the Queen of England.

Queen Catherine summoned the attractive, extremely intelligent Vives to her court, and he soon became the tutor to her young daughter, the Princess Mary. With this limited experience Vives wrote on a topic rarely mentioned in the 1500's, the education of women. This work was a startling novelty to King Henry VIII and others in authority.

Vives' Spanish origin and his writings ultimately led to his exile from England, and he fled to Bruges in Belgium, where he produced his greatest work in the field of education, *De Tradendis Disciplinis.*

In this volume, Vives discusses many things; higher education, moral training, language teaching, and the relationship of schools to life. Juan Luis also made many contributions in formulating the laws of memory and forgetting. It is because of the *De Tradendis Disciplinis* that Vives is now regarded as the "founder of educational psychology."

With regard to method, Vives should be remembered for the inductive process of learning, although he acknowledged its use by Aristotle and others who lived centuries before him. Francis Bacon (1561-1626) is generally regarded as the founder of the inductive method, although Bacon's *Novum Organum* was published a century after Vives' time. The inductive method simply defined is the grouping of certain cases or particular instances from which a general rule is derived. Vives proposed induction not as a teaching method but as a means of discovering new scientific principles.

Vives advocated a special method in the study of foreign languages. Known as "the double translation," this method required the student to translate a Latin passage into the vernacular and later to translate the modern language back into the classical. Vives maintained that a student comprehended far more of a given language by this dual process of translation to and from his native tongue. Later, Roger Ascham (1515-1568) was a staunch advocate of the "double translation" as a method of teaching.

It was during the period of Vives' productive life that the religious upheaval known as the Protestant Revolution (or Reformation) occurred, sparked by the posting of the ninety-five theses by Martin Luther on the doors of the Schlosskirche in Wittenberg on October 31, 1517.

This Revolution brought not only religious arguments but political battles as well. In fact, only four years after the proclamation of the ninety-five theses, the bloody battle and siege of Pamplona was waged. It was during this battle that a certain Spanish nobleman, Ignatius of Loyola, was gravely wounded.

During the extended time of his convalescence, Ignatius read books on the life of Christ and the lives of the saints, and eventually began to think seriously of becoming a priest. On August 15, 1534, Ignatius of Loyola accompanied six companions in the recitation of vows which started the Society of Jesus. Although others have looked upon them as a body of shock troops or the nucleus of a fanatical army to stamp out heresy, this small group of initial Jesuits actually banded together for mutual spiritual aid. Their first plan was to go to Jerusalem to convert the infidel in accordance with Ignatius' *Spiritual Exercises.* They promised, though, that if this did not work within a year, they would go to Rome and let the Pope decide what he wanted them to do. The Pope asked these first Jesuits to assume the leadership of several colleges.

The influence of these Jesuit priests began to be felt within a short time. In the lifetime of their saintly founder, colleges were established in such places as Messina, Palermo, Naples, Gandia, Salamanca, Valencia, Burgos, Saragossa, Lisbon, and Vienna. It has been reported that over two thousand students were enrolled at their Roman College by 1584 and that, by 1615, the Jesuits were conducting 373 colleges.

This widespread educational system soon produced a uniform method of teaching which ultimately led to the development of the *Ratio Studiorum.*

Ignatius himself did not compose the *Ratio;* in fact, it was not written until long after his death. Nevertheless, the *Ratio Studiorum* was based upon the Constitutions of the Society of Jesus which St. Ignatius had written about 1550 after ten years of meditation and work. The *Ratio* was actually the work of many men and institutions and stands today as one of the greatest examples of curriculum construction.

The many drafts and revisions of the *Ratio* required over
fifty years of compilation and would require a considerable
digression to narrate fully.[1] For our purposes, the method
contained within the *Ratio* is the most important aspect to
be explored.

Although the Scholastic method of teaching was primarily
used at the outset in the Jesuit schools, the publication of
the *Ratio* introduced a standard approach to the instruction
and organization of classes, and ultimately to the Jesuit
method of teaching which has survived to this day.

For illustration, let us imagine ourselves at the College
of Valencia, the town of Vives' birth, where Father Alfredo
Herrera, S.J., is teaching a Latin class. (The accompanying
diagram depicts the classroom arrangement.)

Father Herrera is seated on a raised platform in front of
the class (Fr. H.). He has chosen Pedro (P) and Sancho (S)
to sit at the foot of his desk as monitors for the lesson. They
were selected because they have currently mastered their
lessons better than any other students. The remaining students are divided into two opposing teams and seated at
tables on either side of the room.

Father Herrera begins the lesson by slowly reading the
first twenty-five lines of Vergil's *Aeneid*. The students listen
attentively.

Father Herrera now reads the passage a second time—
slowly, so the students may take notes. Then follows a grammatical analysis of the passage wherein difficult words and
terms are picked out and explained in detail to the students.
Father Herrera also correlates the lesson with historical
events occurring in Vergil's time. Once Father Herrera is

---

[1] For the interested reader, Robert Schwickerath's *Jesuit Education* (St.
Louis: B. Herder Book Co., 1904), and Alan P. Farrell's *The Jesuit Code of
Liberal Education* (Milwaukee: Bruce Publishing Co., 1938), give detailed
accounts of the many transitions and vicissitudes which the early editions of
the *Ratio Studiorum* passed through.

THE JESUIT METHOD — CLASSROOM PLAN

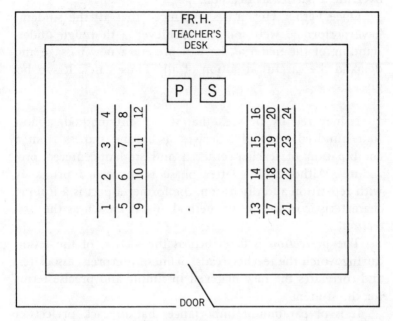

certain that the students understand the passage, he tells them to memorize specific lines or sections. He also instructs them to write a homework composition about the lines they have learned.

The next morning, the students assemble and Pedro and Sancho check attendance. Pedro now calls on student #1 from his side of the room and Sancho picks student #16 from the opposite side to repeat parts of yesterday's lesson. Father Herrera, as the master, presides while the monitors continue to question and judge various students on their individual performances. Often cross-discussions and disputations arise as the students interact and exchange their thoughts on those twenty-five lines of Vergil. Although Pedro and Sancho are striving to record fair grades and to act as impartial judges so that they may retain their monitorial positions of honor, Father Herrera will often interrupt and overrule a particular decision.

Once Father Herrera is convinced that all the students have performed well and have achieved a thorough understanding of the material, he will present a new passage and demand the careful attention of all. Thus a new lesson begins.

It may readily be seen that this Jesuit method, almost four hundred years old, derives its lasting success from a combination of teacher-centered and student-centered procedures. Although the latter phase is concerned primarily with repetition and discussion, the former aspect is a unique characteristic of the Jesuit method and is known as the *prelection*.

The *prelection* is described as the section of the lesson during which the teacher reads, defines, interprets, associates, and correlates the new material in simple and precise terms for the student.

It is of paramount importance that in each prelection the teacher thoroughly explain and analyze a particular author's text completely *before* any supplementary work is assigned to the student.

As seen in the lesson of Father Herrera, the emphasis of the *Ratio* is upon *a little matter perfectly known,* rather than much information vaguely grasped and poorly retained.

The basic objective of each prelection is to dispose the student to profitable self-activity with adequate motivation, which ultimately results in the student's clear and forceful presentation in imitation of the classical author as well as original literary creations.

These are the specific parts considered necessary for an effective use of the Jesuit method.

1. *Prelection* is the *sine qua non* of the Jesuit procedure. The initial phase of the lesson begins with the introduction

of a passage chosen by the teacher. Once the lines or paragraphs of the selection have been presented, the teacher analyzes the matter in this manner:

a. *reading*—the passage is read through once without interruption; then it is read again at a speed permitting students to transcribe notes.

b. *translation*—the teacher slowly explains the meaning of the passage in the language of the learner.

c. *analysis*—word by word and line by line, the teacher carefully breaks down the content in respect to grammatical and rhetorical construction, as well as meaningful interpretation.

d. *association*—by correlation with history and geography or other related disciplines, the teacher links the new content to past experience.

e. *assignment*—following the teacher's intensive consideration of the new passage, the students are instructed to memorize and creatively describe the content of the prelection.

2. *Repetition* is the result of the prelection and usually takes place on the following day. This phase of the lesson involves three activities on the part of the student:

a. *memoriter*—rote line-for-line repetition of the actual content of the new passage, which the monitors are required to exact from each individual in the classroom. (Modern practice often omits the use of monitors and has the teacher listen to each student's recitation.)

b. *concertatio*—the discussion and disputation among the students of the meaning of the passage under consideration. Much of the interpretation and analysis which the teacher had presented on the previous day is expected to be recalled and related in this creative interchange.

c. *emulation* — after successful recitations or debates, prizes or rewards are often given to the best students. It should also be noted that the Jesuits carefully grade students' compositions and give tests at the end of each week. Monitors for the following week's lessons are selected on the basis of these tests. This system of emulation—or reward for outstanding scholastic performance—is an essential feature of the Jesuit procedure.

Another aspect of the award system of Jesuit education is the establishment of "academies" which are associations of outstanding students assigned to do further work and specialized research. Such a designation of particularly capable pupils is commonly known today as an Honors Program.

Today the Jesuit method of instruction lends itself to classroom use with the same versatility that has characterized it since Father Herrera's time. A lesson in theology, philosophy, Latin, English, French, or any foreign language can very satisfactorily be presented in this framework.

For purposes of contemporary interpretation, here is an example that might be found in an English literature lesson planned according to the Jesuit method for a modern high school class. To begin his *prelection,* the teacher reads these famous lines from Shakespeare's *Julius Caesar*:

> (*Reading*)
>
> ANTHONY: Friends, Romans, countrymen, lend me
> your ears;
> I come to bury Caesar, not to praise him.
> The evil that men do lives after them;
> The good is oft interred with their bones;
> So let it be with Caesar.

(*Rereading*)

The teacher now slowly repeats the above.

(*Translation*)

The teacher might adapt the passage into modern speech in this manner:

> Friends, fellow citizens, countrymen, let me have
> your attention;
> I have come here to bury Caesar, not to praise him.

The evil that men do still has its effects after they
    have died;
The good, however, is often buried with them;
Let this, too, be the case with Caesar.

(Analysis)

In discussing the artistic and rhetorical style of the passage, the teacher will now introduce the metaphor as exemplified by the words "lend me your ears." The meaning of personification, too, could be illustrated by the use of the word *evil*: "The evil that men do lives after them." The vocabulary word "inter" would also be defined.

(Association)

For the next step, the teacher associates or relates this passage to poems that the students have read during the year which also contained metaphors and personifications. In addition, the historical times and struggles of Caesar and Antony might be recalled and correlated to the lines under consideration.

(Assignment)

At this point, the teacher might remind the students of the importance of memorizing the new selection. He might also assign a composition on this topic: "Why do you think it is true that the good a person does is often buried with him, whereas the evil he has committed continues to have its effect long after his death?"

On the following day the students are expected to offer *repetition* of what has been taught in the prelection by:

(Memoriter)

Oral recitation of the "Friends, Romans" speech by individual students selected at random.

(Concertatio)

Open disputation by the students on such topics as the one presented in their composition or perhaps personification, metaphor, good and evil deeds, or any phase of the lesson analyzed in the prelection.

(Emulation)

The teacher might suggest that the student who masters all of the week's passages to the highest degree of perfection will be awarded a ticket to a local production of Shakespeare.

A similar form of reward might be to appoint the best student to judge the recitations of the others, in the manner of a monitor.

SUMMARY

Repetitio est mater studiorum (Repetition is the mother of studies) is an often quoted principle of Jesuit education. As practiced in the method of the *Ratio,* repetition is indeed a vital ingredient of learning. Through repetition, the student may focus upon and grasp the most important essentials of the particular lesson being presented. Many aspects which may have been missed by a single reading or lecture are mastered by repetition.

Not only do the students repeat, however; but they must also listen, summarize, apply, and discuss throughout the course of the lesson. In this way, many avenues of active learning are opened to the student, while the teacher is also required through the prelection to present the material from many aspects.

This method also imparts a broad overview to the learner. In addition to solving the many subproblems which may be related to the overall topic, the general prelection also prevents digressions.

The Jesuit method of instruction, however, naturally has certain disadvantages. The award system or emulation pattern, although it creates interest and competition, will often favor a few bright students, while poorer ones may become discouraged. Because not all the students can always be kept happy, discipline problems may develop.

Since this method requires such thorough examination

and mastery of the material, it generally allows only a few subjects to be taught and consequently becomes too restrictive in modern classrooms. In addition, some subjects—such as the sciences—are not well suited to this method and should hardly ever be attempted by this procedure. Employed only when it can be most effective, the Jesuit method can form an integral part of a flexible teaching program.

9. THE VINCENTIAN METHOD

It is very simple . . . just nature, motives, and means.

While it is true that the founding of the Society of Jesus and the publication of the *Ratio Studiorum* contributed greatly to education and especially to renovation within the Church, many abuses still remained. The Council of Trent (1545-1562) was called chiefly as an attempt to remedy the prevailing conditions.

One of the major problems faced by the bishops who convened at Trent was the renewal of spiritual life within the Church. The Council particularly decried the inadequate education of the clergy. Up until that time, such training merely required that an interested candidate should reside in a cathedral rectory, pursue the necessary liturgical procedures, and learn the dogmatic and moral theology by informal observation. There was neither a definite training period nor a required course of study. The progress of a candidate usually depended on the amount of time which his bishop or a designated priest could devote to such a master-apprentice relationship.

More than fifty years passed after the adjournment of the Tridentine Council, however, before genuine reform was achieved in the education of the clergy. It was St. Vincent de Paul (1580-1660) who introduced formal seminary training for priests at the College des Bons-Enfants in Paris when he established his Congregation of the Mission in 1625.

Although he was one of the most renowned reformers and leading national figures of his time, Vincent de Paul was not a member of the aristocracy. Born to a farming family in 1580, Vincent was intelligent and well schooled. He studied in Spain and for seven years at Toulouse; he was then trained by the Bishop of Tarbes and, in 1600, at the age of twenty, was ordained to the priesthood.

In 1605 he traveled to Marseilles and, en route home, was wounded by Turkish pirates and taken to Tunis. Sold as a slave to an African fisherman and later to an aged alchemist, Vincent ultimately was assigned to serve an apostate Christian from Nice. After some time as this man's slave, Vincent impressed the man's wife so much by his piety that she helped him to escape back to France. Having tasted suffering, slavery, and poverty, Vincent developed an exceptional understanding and compassion for the poor.

Shortly after his return to his native France, he was appointed chaplain to the General of the Gallies, Phillippe Emmanuel de Gondi. A dying farmer on the de Gondi estate made a general confession of his sins and declared publicly that he had rectified many bad confessions of the past because of the insight and understanding of Father Vincent.

Madame de Gondi was most impressed and exclaimed that, if a man like the farmer—whom everyone regarded as good—was in such great need of a good and complete confession, how much more must others be in such need! Consequently, Madame de Gondi begged Father Vincent to give a mission to the people on her estates. The result was that so many people wanted to make general confessions that St. Vincent had to call in other priests, including the Jesuits, to assist him.

During the next few years, Vincent and several other secular priests continued to give missions for the people in that area. Often Vincent became disheartened, however, to discover that, in spite of the transitory reform induced by the missions, the people were lapsing back into sin because they did not have a zealous, well-trained secular clergy. This realization prompted Vincent, with the help of the de Gondis, to establish a "seminary" in order to formalize instruction for the priesthood. The College des Bons-Enfants and the Priory of St. Lazare were used for this purpose. Thus began the Congregation of the Mission.

Although Vincent de Paul founded the seminary initially to preserve the good work of his own congregation, the tremendous effectiveness of such training was soon recognized and the secular clergy were also instructed at St. Lazare and other seminaries which were founded later.

However, St. Vincent is remembered most of all for his great charity to the poor, the sick, and the imprisoned. In this regard, he is responsible for bringing religious sisters out from the cloister into the streets to help and teach the poor. With St. Louise de Marillac, St. Vincent founded the Daughters of Charity, the largest community in the Roman Catholic Church today.

In addition to all these significant innovations and contributions to the religious life, Vincent de Paul has also left a method of teaching of inestimable value. It was his desire that the priests of his Congregation of the Mission preach the Gospel in imitation of the way Christ Himself had taught the people—simply and sincerely.

At the time of St. Vincent far too many sermons tended to be pompous and pedantic. It was the fashion of the day for sermons to be presented in a polished style, even though the faithful frequently did not understand the grand references or erudite terms.

St. Vincent was uneasy with this approach and consequently declared that preachers should strive not so much to polish their sentences as to save souls. Against such pretentious eloquence, Vincent set his *Petite Methode* which consisted in preaching only the Gospel, but preaching it from the heart. St. Vincent did not fear to assert that his method was inspired by God, not by men, because it was the very method used by Jesus Christ and His Apostles. St. Vincent attached great importance to his "Little Method" because he had learned by experience the great necessity of explaining doctrine according to the capacity of the listeners—the poor of the countryside, the city, the prisons, and the gallies as well. But, as he expressly says, such a method is valid for all sorts of audiences and for all circumstances, even in the towns, even in Paris—for truth must be the end of all processes of the mind.

Of all these settings, however, St. Vincent was probably most happy in the simple chapel of St. Lazare. In this dim, candlelit center of the Congregation of the Mission, St. Vincent softly preached the Word of God. The dark wooden benches reflected the flickering candles, and the learned priests and eager seminarians must have been impressed with the complete simplicity and sincerity of their leader. Robed in a plain black cassock under a long, flowing surplice, St. Vincent would begin in a style like this:

"Thanksgiving to God is one of the most important acts we may render. By giving thanks to God, we acknowledge our complete dependence upon Him and show our gratitude for the life He gave us and the way He sustains our lives each day. By thanking God, we tell Him that we truly appreciate all His goodness to us.

"Thanksgiving to God is very necessary. Without God, we cannot do anything. We must therefore tell Him how thankful we are for all the many blessings we have, or else we would be very ungrateful children. Just as we certainly would not take a good friend for granted, so also we would never want to fail in showing our appreciation to our Best Friend.

"How may we, so unworthy, give thanks to God? Perhaps the best way is to remember what a good Father He is to all of us. Let us use the word FATHER to help with our thanksgiving.

"F is for faith. Tell God how fervently you believe all the truths He has revealed.

"A is for adoration. Try to express your profound

adoration to the Almighty, All-Knowing, and All-Loving God.

"T is for thanking God for all the good things He has given us and all those we love.

"H is for the humility we must feel as we talk to God. Only when we realize how very much we need God can we truly appreciate how insufficient we are by ourselves.

"E is for entreaty. In thanking God for His goodness, we also need to beg His continued blessings. Remember He said, 'Ask and you shall receive.' Let us not forget that we shall always need His help.

"R is for the resolution we should make to be more pleasing to God. Now is the time to promise God that, by our actions, we shall try to show how thankful we are for His great goodness."

A simple, direct, and straight-forward presentation—these are the basic characteristics of the "little method" of St. Vincent de Paul.

In order to achieve this concise yet thorough treatment of a topic, three distinct steps must be followed.

1. *Nature.* This is the initial phase of the lesson during which the teacher describes, in the language of the listener, the nature or characteristics of the topic. When St. Vincent spoke of the importance of thanksgiving to his listeners, he was presenting the nature of the matter. This is *what* is being studied.

2. *Motive.* In this part of the lesson, the teacher describes the reasons *why* the particular topic is being considered. This is a motivation for the learners, as St. Vincent gave in telling why thanksgiving is necessary.

3. *Means.* These are the final parts of the lesson which express *how* the topic may be learned or put into practice. Actual ways of retaining the subject matter, through formulas or rules, are given at this point. Often a mnemonic device, such as "FATHER," or other alliterative or "clue" techniques, can be employed in assisting the memory, although they are not an integral part of this method.

St. Vincent also advised the use of concrete objects to illustrate the nature, motive, or means of a lesson. In fact, he explicitly told the Daughters of Charity to use pictures and figures to describe the lessons of catechism to little children. Vincent de Paul encouraged the sisters to use Nativity scenes to demonstrate to the children the main characters of Bethlehem and the various men and animals present at the first Christmas. Johann Comenius (1592-1670) is frequently regarded as the originator of this technique in his *Orbis Sensualium Pictus* (1654), but it is to St. Vincent and his "little method" that some of the credit for this innovation must be given.

The utility of this method can readily be recognized. Although St. Vincent devised it to preach how to lead a good life and practice virtue, the "little method" is by no means restricted to theology or philosophy.

History, geography, literature, mathematics, science, even the learning of foreign languages and the spelling of words, can be most effectively taught by this Vincentian method, from the early grades through college and throughout life.

As long as the topic consists of a term, place, method, process, or form whose nature can be described and explained, it remains the teacher's task to motivate and devise the best means for learning.

A lesson on patriotism—*what* it is to be patriotic, *why* we should be patriotic, and *how* we can develop into patriotic citizens—could be skillfully devised and delivered by the "little method."

Another example might be a scientific study of the phases of the moon as outlined in this way.

1. NATURE: *What* are the eight phases of the moon and the shapes that appear with each phase.

2. MOTIVE: *Why* our class should understand the changes the moon undergoes. It can readily be seen how vital it is to be aware of the many characteristics of our universe.

3. MEANS: *How* we can understand the phases by learning that the moon's light is reflected from the sun as the moon revolves around the earth. Models of the sun, earth, and moon can help the students to see clearly these changes in the moon's lighted portion as each month progresses.

Thus this what-why-how method of St. Vincent can be adapted by a twentieth-century teacher with the same ease and facility that St. Vincent intended his Congregation to have when he imparted the Word of God.

SUMMARY

Preaching to the poor, reform of the clergy, organizing the seminary, the foundation of the Congregation of the Mission and the Daughters of Charity, and the practice of the "little method"—these are but a part of the lasting contribution of St. Vincent de Paul to the progress of education.

St. Vincent himself was a great teacher not only because of his method, but because of his manner. The imitation of Christ was his goal and the goal he set for all the Vincentians who would follow in his mission.

St. Vincent truly taught by his good example—he was a living model of charity, patience, humility, understanding, and goodness. The practice of these qualities should be the aim of every good teacher.

The Vincentian method itself has a vast potential in many teaching situations. The childlike simplicity of approach establishes and confirms rapport and prevents confusion and frustration. This direct what-why-how procedure also helps to keep the teacher on the point of the lesson.

Of course, the danger naturally arises that a teacher might attempt to overuse this method and endeavor to compartmentalize all knowledge in this framework. If all lessons were set in this pattern, experimentation and creativity would naturally be stifled.

It is important to note, however, that almost all teachers use the "little method," or variations of it, although very frequently they are not conscious that they are doing so.

Essentially, all lessons contain a substance or nature and it is generally the teacher's task to help the students to learn how to master this material. Strong motivations in the form of pictures, demonstrations, and films, are often the techniques used to secure the learner's attention and response.

Therefore, even though it is not formalized in many instances, the "little method" is present in most good lessons to some degree.

10. THE MENTAL DISCIPLINE METHOD

It matters little what a child studies . . . so long as he does not like it. LOCKE

A method that is not a method. Is there such a thing? If there is, how do we handle it in a book on methodology? Unfortunately, there is such a thing and it is extremely difficult to describe.

In approaching the latter half of the seventeenth century, we discover a teaching method which cannot be outlined in exactly the same manner as the previously described methods. Known as mental discipline, this method, like all methods, aims for the development of the intellect. However, mental discipline is unique because it is not so much a technique or procedure as a theory about reaching the learning goal.

Defined as the method by which a particular subject is regarded as a discipline of human powers developed by orderly exercise, mental discipline has probably existed since the first school or prescribed curriculum. However, John Locke (1632-1704) is generally recognized as the chief modern proponent of such a theory, although it was not original with him.

Educated at Westminster and Oxford, Locke earned his master's degree in 1658. He taught Greek, rhetoric, and philosophy at Oxford from 1660 to 1664. In later years, he served as a private tutor to the sons of the nobility. The theories he gradually developed during these years of teaching were published in 1693 as *Some Thoughts Concerning Education.*

Locke was an aristocrat and no advocate of democracy. Essentially, he believed that only gentlemen need be educated, and this process should be in a tutorial relationship. "For if those of that rank are by their education once set right, they will quickly bring all the rest into order."[1]

In his theory of education for the upper classes, Locke combined ideas from many other scholars. He revived Aristotle's concept of the mind as a *tabula rasa,* a "blank or erased tablet," thus emphasizing the potentiality of the intellect. Just as grooves and figures are carved into a wax tablet, so also ideas can make impressions on that unique faculty of a student known as his intellect. The more often or sharper the impression is made, the easier the intellect finds it to make distinctions and to operate effectively.

Besides the concept of the *tabula rasa,* Locke borrowed other ideas about the intellect and memory. Many men have recommended that a particular subject be learned not because of its pragmatic or utilitarian value but because of the mental exercise provided by the experience. They held that the mind is made up of sections or compartments and, just as one trains a bodily muscle by repeated use, so also the mental faculties were thought to be trained by repetition.

In this regard, it is axiomatic that when a particular subject area falls into disfavor, its teachers advocate that the subject be retained in the curriculum—not because of its intrinsic worth, but because of the training it provides for the mind. Such teachers naturally want to retain their positions, but they also claim that these subjects, which possess

---

[1] John Locke, *Some Thoughts Concerning Education* (Cambridge: Cambridge University Press, 1880), p. 3.

no apparent usefulness, provide more exercise or discipline for the mental faculties. This discipline and development of the intellect or memory can later serve as a means of transfer in practical situations.

Following this theory of formal discipline, Locke taught that the subject a student learns is not as important as the fact that he learns it. In other words, Locke viewed the discipline of the mind received in the learning process as paramount to the curriculum content.

Locke further declared, "As the strength of the body lies chiefly in being able to endure hardship, so also does that of the mind." The more difficult a topic is to grasp, the stronger the mind will be once the topic is finally mastered. Or, we might say, it matters little what a child studies so long as he does not like it!

The greater the difficulty or aversion which Locke's students displayed toward a particular subject, e.g., Latin, Greek, or Sanskrit, the better their minds were trained once they thoroughly understood their lessons. It was not that Locke wanted his boys to become experts in communicating in Latin or Greek, but instead he aimed to develop their intellects by such challenging yet unappealing exercises. They were learning for the sake of learning.

John Locke's mental discipline method is not a method in the sense that certain procedures and steps can be set down for use by the modern teacher. Mental discipline is much more a philosophy than a specific method of teaching. A teacher who advocates this theory of learning would direct all his teaching in a framework of transfer rather than plan an occasional lesson labeled "mental discipline approach."

In discussing mathematics—not for practical application, but for mental discipline—Locke wrote, "I have mentioned mathematics, as a way to settle in the mind a habit of reasoning closely and in train; not that I think it necessary that all men should be deep mathematicians, but that having got the way of reasoning, which that study necessarily brings the mind to, they might be able to transfer it to other parts of knowledge as they shall have occasion."[2]

Thus a teacher using mental discipline hopes to achieve transfer of learning and clear thinking more than specific content mastery. It is the judgments and reasoning that a student derives from studying algebraic or geometric concepts which are sought in such a case, so that the student might exercise and develop the faculties to think and act intelligently in complex matters of adult life.

Such transfer of training has been discussed extensively in today's educational literature, not only with regard to classical languages, mathematical reasoning, and logic, but even in such practical fields as the nursing arts.[3]

In many cases, teachers make use of the principles of mental discipline, although they are not particularly aware of the fact. While students in such a situation will develop new insights to a certain degree, success in strengthening intellectual capacities is far greater when the teacher consciously teaches for the transfer of a specific goal or skill.

However, there is no particular method or procedure for the teacher to employ even if he wishes to achieve transfer. Consequently, any of the previously discussed methods—lecture, memorization, discussion, and parable—can be fashioned to present material in a manner conducive to direct intellectual stimulation and exercise for its own sake.

[2] John Locke, "Of the Conduct of the Understanding," in *The Philosophical Works of John Locke,* edited by J. A. St. John (London: George Bell and Sons, 1905), p. 44.

[3] There is an excellent treatment of transfer of training in John M. Stephens, *The Psychology of Classroom Learning* (New York: Holt, Rinehart and Winston, 1965). For a fine illustration of a thorough study of one subject area, see Margaret E. Courtney, "The Effectiveness of the Classroom Laboratory in the Teaching of Nursing Arts," *Nursing Research,* Summer 1959, pp. 148-54.

SUMMARY

Whether or not mental discipline should be classified as a method of instruction is a question which ultimately depends on one's definition of method. Many scholars would argue that Locke's mental discipline theory is a method in the fullest sense. Some even go so far as to assign subjects according to a descending order of difficulty: mathematics, then Latin, then grammar, and so on. The danger naturally arises that subjects then tend to become categorized as to their usefulness in developing the mind. Actually, mental discipline seems to be more the philosophy behind the utilization of a particular subject area rather than a bona fide technique for teaching, which would be necessary according to our definition of method.

That there is a disciplinary element necessary to education we cannot deny, but that it is not as important as its extreme advocates claim—nor as unimportant as its opponents contend—is the common sense conclusion that must be reached.

Mental discipline is a valid approach when teachers maintain a moderate realism in its use in the total curriculum. The disciplinary value of a subject like Latin, with its precise rules and cases of agreement, cannot be denied, but one should not attempt to teach only those subjects that impart such exercise. The ability to think is vital, but not all learning can be transferred or applied to every situation. Specific studies for their own sake are essential in developing the complete individual.

Mental discipline is at its best, therefore, when one endeavors to prepare the student to think, to reason, and to use his faculties independently in untried and challenging situations.

11. THE SELF-ACTIVITY
AND SENSE REALISM
METHODS

. . . the words command and obey should have no place in his dictionary. ROUSSEAU

Educational methods, like most procedures in life, are often downgraded as vehemently as they are defended. It is usually extreme use which produces the greatest disfavor for teaching methods, and so it was with the formal mental discipline approach. By the dawn of the eighteenth century, Locke's theory had been reduced in practice to nothing more than rigid memorization of theories and formulas, the exact opposite of the intellectual development he set forth as its goal.

This regimented denial of freedom and individual thought, coupled with the spirit of Romanticism which was beginning to pervade Europe, provided fertile ground for the seed of progressivism to emerge.

As personified by its chief exponent, Jean Jacques Rousseau (1712-1778), progressivism was characterized by the free and unencumbered expression of feeling and emotion.

Rousseau did not believe in being restricted in any way. He freely expressed his love for many women and consequently fathered several illegitimate children. As the children grew, he sent them to orphanages but then became concerned about their education. Since he was distressed about the restrictive procedures of the period, Rousseau decided to set forth his own educational theory in *Émile* (1762).

Émile represented one of his own sons, and Rousseau explained the manner in which he would train the boy according to progressive philosophy. The first sentence of *Émile* gives the essence of Rousseau's claim: "All things are good as they come out of the hands of their Creator but everything degenerates in the hands of men."[1] In so denying the doctrine of original sin, Rousseau further declared that it is society which corrupts and defiles human nature. He then concluded that the best education would necessarily exclude the influence of society, i.e., the child must be left alone and not guided or restricted in any way.

For Rousseau, the ideal man was not Aristotle, Pliny, or Buffon, but Robinson Crusoe because he provided for himself in the realm of pure nature. The Indians in the New World were likewise idealized by Rousseau as "noble savages" because they were educated in the pure state of nature. He believed that if his Émile could be left to nature, he would then be like these "noble savages."

Obviously, Rousseau was not only rebelling against the discipline and formalized learning of previous years, but he was also attempting to turn aside centuries of scholarly thought for his "return to nature."

In order to achieve the training he desired for Émile, Rousseau set forth definite principles and theories. "The words *command* and *obey* should have no place in his dictionary, much less those of duty and obligation. . . ."[2]

Rousseau also advocated complete spontaneity of action. In fact he went further to say, "The only habit in which a child should be indulged is that of contracting none. . . ."[3]

[1] Jean Jacques Rousseau, *Émile*, trans. Barbara Foxley (London: J. M. Dent and Sons, Ltd., 1911), p. 1.

[2] *Ibid.*, p. 65.

[3] *Ibid.*, p. 29.

If Rousseau could have had his way, he would have taken an infant, fenced him off from the rest of the family, and periodically delivered food over the fence. The child would have had complete independence of action and would have learned to solve all his problems simply and naturally.

If such a method were carried to the extreme or "ideal" (as Rousseau would have called it), the teacher would become nothing but a custodian. The natural interest of the child is all that is important; if there is no inner drive, feeling, or inclination to learn a particular subject, then a student cannot be expected to give such a subject the perseverance necessary to success. The child must have complete freedom; he should do only what he wants to do. In effect, then, the only method for Rousseau is no method at all, other than the self-activity of the child.

Rousseau's revolutionary ideas were hailed by fellow Romanticists. Many, in fact, tried to put these theories into actual practice. Johann Bernhard Basedow (1723-1790) opened one of the first German schools founded solely on this principle of natural freedom. After a short time, however, the Philanthropinum, as Basedow called the school he founded at Dessau, collapsed completely. Although some writers try to ascribe this failure to Basedow's inability as a teacher, it was this theory of complete permissiveness which proved the greatest liability in the experiment.

Still another exponent of this liberal approach to education was Johann Heinrich Pestalozzi (1746-1827). A member of a middle-class Zurich family, Pestalozzi initially studied for the ministry, later turned to law, and finally chose agriculture.

He and his wife lived on a one-hundred-acre farm at Neuhof. Much impressed by Rousseau's writings, Pestalozzi attempted to operate a school for poor children, and, although the school was also far from successful, his efforts influenced many. Expanding greatly on Rousseau's theory of self-activity, Pestalozzi emphasized the importance of sensory perception in learning.

Although, centuries before, Aristotle and St. Thomas Aquinas had both stated that nothing reaches the intellect unless it is first perceived by the senses, Pestalozzi actually put this theory into practice in teaching little children.

Calling his procedure the method of sense realism, Pestalozzi taught by showing a certain object to his students. After they were given time to perceive the various characteristics of the object, then he would tell the children what the object was called. He would "show" and then "tell" about each new concept. In this way, Pestalozzi used the physical or concrete to achieve the intellectual or abstract. This procedure inherently required much activity on the part of the children in sensing and perceiving and, hence, adherence to Rousseau's plea for individual self-activity.

Pestalozzi produced two books, *Leonard and Gertrude* and *How Gertrude Teaches Her Children*. Basically, he expounded on the notions of Rousseau in regard to the natural capacites of man, but he also explained that a student cannot learn merely by his own particular wish or desire. To Pestalozzi, the importance of the teacher rested in creating lively sense impressions to stimulate learning. Such learning, he asserted, should be the goal for every child. Pestalozzi wrote, "The instruction she [Gertrude] gave them in the rudiments of arithmetic was intimately connected with the realities of life."

Although we remember Pestalozzi as the father of the method of sense realism, his greatest impact lies chiefly in his overall influence on modern educational development.

By teaching poor children, Pestalozzi propagated the democratic idea of education. He provided an impetus for the democratic society that was emerging during his lifetime, rather than any new or startling theories. For Pestalozzi, the important goal was the full development of the powers of every human being.

Pestalozzi tried to inspire all people about education. He emphasized group management in the classroom, not the tutorial relationships advocated by so many of the theorists before him. Pestalozzi's method was not unique or original (the Brothers of the Christian Schools under St. John Baptist de la Salle [1651-1719] had already initiated group work and a simultaneous method), but his democratizing of the framework and procedure of learning was.

To achieve this overall democratic influence in the classroom, Pestalozzi aimed to give each student an equal opportunity to perceive and learn. The teacher was first to present the concrete objects for each child to see, feel, and examine. Then the object would be identified verbally by its particular title or name.

In this way, Pestalozzi's method of sense realism can be divided into two necessary steps, labeled simply (1) show and (2) tell.

To utilize this show-and-tell procedure in the most effective way, Pestalozzi sought to categorize all sense impressions into three groups.

1. *Language.* The possession of the fundamentals of sound and words provides means of self-expression in language form. Sound is acquired by development of the child's speech organs. Next, words are learned by name teaching. Here are included names of important objects of history, geography, and nature. To learn these, Pestalozzi suggested that the children view a river valley from some vantage point. Afterward, he suggested that the children bring back samples of the soil from that valley and its surrounding hills with which they would build their own relief map. When this was completed the children would be shown a professional map of the same territory. This map now "made sense" to them. This approach is similar to a modern field trip.

2. *Form*. Pestalozzi's second basic element of education had three subdivisions:

(a) measuring—this is a sense impression differing from the ordinary in that it is similar to an organized experience. By continually measuring and comparing, one is able to recognize proportions and make correct judgments about height and weight.

(b) drawing—Pestalozzi insisted on the drawing of real objects so that shading and perspective might be more thoroughly learned.

(c) writing—Pestalozzi also encouraged drawing as a preliminary to learning to write because it makes writing easier and gives accuracy and precision to the written word. In teaching writing, Pestalozzi stresses viewing the letter in its correct form and size, practicing each part of the letter, and then joining all the parts together to form the correct letter.

3. *Number*. Pestalozzi's third means of acquiring knowledge provides directness and clarifies ideas by presenting the children with the objects to be counted, added, and subtracted. He felt that the child must understand that two and three means two balls and three balls or two apples and three apples. Pestalozzi maintained that the child cannot understand two and three in the abstract; he must see them in reality.

In today's schools, disks, sticks, felt materials, and real objects are used to illustrate problems before solutions are found.

In each of these three categories—language, form, and number—Pestalozzi used the physical to achieve the intellectual. This simple principle of learning is the essence of his method or procedure. It was not new—it was simply the democratization of a centuries-old ideal.

Activity became an essential classroom ingredient, not only for the teacher but also for each individual student. This was no mere recitation or rote memory attempt. Everyone had to learn to feel, act, and think for himself. Skillful group management and careful preparation by the teacher became vital.

Today the Pestalozzian approach is used most successfully in the kindergarten and elementary grades. In many cases, the very concept of show and tell is presented not only by the teacher but by individual students as well.

The basic foundation of this method of sense realism rests, of course, upon the belief that everything children will need to know can be experienced through the senses. Obviously, however, not every abstract learning can be made concrete.

SUMMARY

That the Pestalozzian influence has left a significant impression on American education cannot be denied. Not only did Pestalozzi apply democratic concepts and theories to teaching, but he also laid the groundwork for much of what we accept as fundamental to our elementary education system today.

Following the inspiration of men like St. Vincent de Paul and Comenius in his *Orbis Sensualium Pictus,* Pestalozzi made concrete materials an integral part of elementary and intermediate grades. Pestalozzi's language-form-number approach of sense realism also firmly rooted elementary science, home economics, geography, and nature study into the course of study.

Sparked by Rousseau's emphasis on individual freedom, Pestalozzi attached new importance to oral expression by his pupils, and teachers had to become more independent of books and better trained at teaching rather than indoctrinating.

Of course the exclusive emphasis Pestalozzi placed on sense realism naturally confines the application of his principles to subjects with concrete matter. Subjects like higher mathematics, philosophy, and theology are automatically excluded from a Pestalozzian-oriented curriculum. In this respect, the method lacks realistic perspective. It is limited to only that which can be perceived empirically.

Such complete dependence on the senses limits intellectual development and prevents any form of pure reasoning and discovery. There is much to be known which human senses cannot perceive directly.

12. THE MONITORIAL SYSTEM

*A new mass-production technique is attempted
in India and England.*

The great impetus given to the democratization of
education did not end with Rousseau and Pestalozzi. In the
years that followed, the teaching of the common people became a major concern. Among the many plans which attempted to provide such schooling for the multitude was the
monitorial system advocated by both Lancaster and Bell.

Before discussing this system of schooling, however, it
might be well to examine the teachings of René Descartes
(1596-1650), whose thoughts were significant in the movement toward mass education.

Through his philosophical and political writings Descartes had inspired the British Revolution of 1688 as much
as Locke and contributed as much as Rousseau in bringing
about the French Revolution of 1789.

Although he is best known in the field of mathematics
for his Cartesian Coordinates in analytical geometry, Descartes is also distinguished for his philosophy of skepticism.
He is further known in the realm of religion where he used
his famous *Cogito, ergo sum* (I think, therefore I am) to
prove his own existence, from which he deduced the existence of God.

It is Descartes' methodology with which we are concerned, however, and it is in this area that he wrote his

famous volume, *Discourse on the Method of Rightly Conducting the Reason and Seeking for Truth in the Sciences.* In this work, Descartes declared that there are four steps in learning.

> The first of these was to accept nothing as true which I did not clearly recognize to be so; that is to say, carefully to avoid precipitation and prejudice in judgments, and to accept in them nothing more than what was presented to my mind so clearly and distinctly that I could have no occasion to doubt it.
>
> The second was to divide up each of the difficulties which I examined into as many parts as possible, and as seemed requisite in order that it might be resolved in the best manner possible.
>
> The third was to carry on my reflections in due order, commencing with objects that were the most simple and easy to understand, in order to rise little by little, or by degrees, to knowledge of the most complex, assuming an order, even if a fictitious one, among those which do not follow a natural sequence relatively to one another.
>
> The last was in all cases to make enumerations so complete and reviews so general that I should be certain of having omitted nothing.[1]

As an illustration of these rules, we could use Descartes' rationalistic approach to the existence of God. He would say:

(1) "In me, there is from time to time the idea of God. Is this idea a true one?"

(2) "Yes, because there must be a cause for everything and hence a cause for my idea of God."

(3) "The cause of everything must be present in the effect in all of its perfections."

[1] René Descartes, *Discourse on the Method of Rightly Conducting the Reason and Seeking for Truth in the Sciences,* as found in Ulich, *Three Thousand Years of Educational Wisdom* (Cambridge, Mass.: Harvard University Press, 1954), p. 319.

(4) "Hence, this must be a true idea and, therefore, God exists."

In our evaluation, Descartes must be regarded as a transitional figure between the ancient and medieval peoples who regarded as valid only that knowledge which could be deduced from general principles and the modern persons who hold that the only valid knowledge is empirical. But to say that Descartes is a transitional figure should not cause anyone to underestimate his impact. The influence of Descartes upon his own time and later ages should not be disregarded. As a matter of fact, the questioning attitude is a good one if it is held in proper balance. But Descartes would have us question everything. This approach to all of life—its truth, its problems, and all its creatures—has been rejected as universal skepticism by most philosophers.

The British, the French, and the American revolutions began with the questioning of the divine right of kings. Once the class system had been broken by the industrial democracy in opposition to the monarchies, the revolutionists also questioned all authority outside their own reason.

With this evolution toward democracy, the people then were to be taught, according to the Jeffersonian ideal, that they must decide on their own leaders. It soon became obvious that the only way to have an intelligent electorate was to have people schooled and taught how to read and write.

Several attempts to provide mass education for the people resulted. One method which was used in the early 1800's was advocated almost simultaneously on opposite ends of the globe.

In 1796, Andrew Bell (1753-1832), who was the superintendent of the Egmore Male Military Academy in Madras, India, developed a mechanical method of instruction in which older children acted as monitors to teach the younger. Joseph Lancaster (1778-1838) opened a school with a similar system of instruction shortly afterward in England. Both men labeled their procedures the "monitorial method" and both procedures were essentially the same. King George III was but one of many Englishmen who lauded this innovation in the schooling of the masses.

As we have already seen, the Jesuits used monitors, but the monitor advocated by the *Ratio Studiorum* was one who followed the classic definition and tended to admonish his fellow pupils. There were usually two in each section and they acted like assistants in the course, grading their sides

THE MONITORIAL SYSTEM

$$M_1 \quad\quad\quad\quad\quad T \quad\quad\quad\quad\quad M_{10}$$
$$M_2 \quad\quad\quad\quad\quad\quad\quad\quad\quad\quad\quad M_9$$
$$M_3 \quad M_4 \quad M_5 \quad M_6 \quad M_7 \quad M_8$$

Step 1: Master teacher instructs monitors.

$$T$$

S S S S S S S S S S	M_1
S S S S S S S S S S	M_2
S S S S S S S S S	M_3
S S S S S S S S S S	M_4
S S S S S S S S S S	M_5
S S S S S S S S S S	M_6
S S S S S S S S S S	M_7
S S S S S S S S S S	M_8
S S S S S S S S S S	M_9
S S S S S S S S S S	M_{10}

Step 2: Each monitor teaches a row of students.

in the competition which the Jesuit system espoused for the advancement of learning.

Lancaster and Bell, however, actually used their monitors as teaching aides. These two men would first teach a fact or concept directly to about eight or ten of the brightest students (or monitors) in the front of the room. These monitors were then expected to return to different rows of about a dozen students each and pass this knowledge on to them.

In this way, each monitor would be in charge of a particular group of students, while the master teacher taught only a small group, the monitors, himself. Thus, although hundreds of students might have been in the same room, instruction was kept individualized to some degree.

Since Lancaster and Bell lived in the era prior to loudspeaker systems and television instruction, the monitorial system seemed to be the only plausible answer to the challenge of mass education.

During this period of political and industrial revolution, monitorial classes were frequently conducted on Sundays because the children worked in factories and textile mills on the other six days of the week. Since it was believed that education was the only way the poor workers could become good citizens and improve their lot, the trend of these original "Sunday Schools" to teach reading, writing, and arithmetic soon became widespread.

Huge halls or dormitories near the factories were generally used as classrooms for these youngsters. A typical lesson might have begun with the master teacher telling all the monitors that $5 + 2 = 7$; each monitor would return to his row and tell his group that $5 + 2 = 7$. Focusing on a particular row, we might have seen the monitor say the arithmetic fact; then each child in the group would be expected to write down $5 + 2 = 7$ on his own slate. The monitor would then instruct all in the row to "show slates," and it would be the monitor's responsibility to check that everyone had written $5 + 2 = 7$ correctly. Once this was done throughout the room, the monitors would return to the master teacher for the next lesson.

This procedure is quite similar to the Pestalozzian show and tell method. Since the eight-year-old who acted as monitor could hardly have been expected to lead his fellow pupils in a discussion or answer questions, he was merely showing or telling new facts to each child in his particular row. More accurately, this method of the monitorial system might be classified as a "tell and retell" approach. The master teacher tells a fact and the monitor retells it to his row of students.

Although the monitorial system of instruction consisted mostly of repetition, drill, and memorization, it did serve a noble purpose in the progress toward universal education. This procedure enabled one teacher to reach one or two hundred students or more instead of the usual several dozen. In the days when teachers were a rarity, this meant that thousands of youngsters, who would have otherwise remained unlettered factory workers, were given an opportunity to improve their position in life.

It is not difficult to see how this method, imported into the United States in the first years of the nineteenth century, was instrumental in expanding rapidly the number of children who could be taught in one school and at a proportionately minimal increase in cost.

But twentieth-century America is a different story. The Lancaster and Bell method, if practiced in the exact format today, would be an outrage in our modern school system. Dependence on mechanical memorization and unqualified children as teachers would negate years of educational progress.

To a modified degree, however, today's teacher can borrow monitorial principles for effective use in the classroom. Mechanical tasks and artistic projects, which often lend themselves to group work, might be an ideal setting for the tell and retell approach.

A primary class, for instance, may be engaged in constructing Mother's Day greetings to take home. The students might be divided into four groups, each working with paper, paste, and paints at different tables. If the teacher desires that the children understand how to cut and fold the paper according to a certain pattern, he could show one student at each table the correct procedure, and, once that child has mastered the format, he could retell about the process to the others. Explanations given by children to children in such cases will often be much clearer than a teacher's general instructions.

Frequently, in group work in arithmetic, for example, the teacher may present a general lesson on addition or subtraction facts. If the work is new, some students will grasp it but others will not. In such a situation, the teacher could attempt to reteach each of the slower pupils individually, or, perhaps better, he could appoint particular students to help others. In this way, the brighter students would not only be helping the others, but they would also be reenforcing their own learning. Of course, such periods of help and practice should be closely supervised by the teacher, who must circulate freely about the room checking each individual's progress.

In the upper grades, such monitorial help might be given by one student to others in biology, chemistry, or physics classes. A certain pupil will often be more adept at performing experiments or demonstrations than others; such a student might very well be called upon to assist four or five others in the laboratory period, when time does not allow the teacher to check each student's work.

Naturally, such a system of helping one's peers should not be overworked. Caution should always be exercised to insure that the brighter students do not lose patience and resort to taking over the entire experiment or project.

SUMMARY

Descartes' theory on the correct method of searching for truth caused many men to question previously accepted knowledge. The monitorial system of Lancaster and Bell gave many who would otherwise not have had it the opportunity to learn to read and write. Although their system was a crude one, it was a logical extension of the simultaneous class arrangement which had begun under St. John Baptist de la Salle.[2] The monitorial schools produced the setting necessary to make literate the great numbers of people who would have otherwise been deprived of all schooling. Once they learned how to read they could proceed toward the goal set by Descartes.

Basically, however, the system was severely inadequate and impractical in its overall contribution to educational methodology. These schools emphasized repetition in the teaching process and treated education purely from the standpoint of routine.

Besides being so mechanical, these monitorial classes deprived the majority of students of contact with qualified teachers. As a result, this system eventually proved, by its inadequacy, that untrained teachers were generally not an asset to a school.

While the monitorial system did meet a great emergency in the growing United States, it was not long before greater resources enabled the people to make larger appropriations for education. For these reasons, the method of Lancaster and Bell had been thoroughly modified or replaced by the beginning of the present century.

---

[2] Jean Baptiste de la Salle (1651-1719), priest of Reims, France, founder of the Brothers of the Christian Schools, began the practice of grouping pupils by achievement level.

13. THE HERBARTIAN
METHOD

---

*Facts are easily explained through reference
to the continual flow of ideas—apperceptive
masses—in our mind.* HERBART

Although Johann Pestalozzi's method of sense realism provided a renewed stimulus to pedagogical progress, there was still much work to be done. The obvious weakness remained that such a procedure failed to assimilate new concepts to old ones. Herein was found a challenge for a new methodology by a young tutor from Oldenburg named Johann Friedrich Herbart (1776-1841).

To master thoroughly the practical aspects of sense realism, Herbart visited Pestalozzi when the latter was teaching at Burgdorf. Sparked by the enthusiastic encouragement of Pestalozzi, Herbart decided to formulate his own experiences as a teacher into certain principles of method, and thought he found the solution in the "apperceptive mass." This is the key expression for an understanding of the Herbartian approach.

Herbart himself was a teacher of philosophy, but he was not regarded as an outstanding educator in his own lifetime. His followers were the ones who eventually popularized the steps to be used in the so-called Herbartian Method.

Although Herbart viewed education as a training for virtue, this virtue was not that which is associated with the divine law or even man's social nature. Morality for him was based on esthetic necessity and was to be obtained by (1) *government*—keeping children occupied all the time; (2) *instruction*—the goal of this phase was the attainment of a "many-sided interest," and (3) *training*—the promotion of a sympathetic understanding between teacher and pupil. Of these three means, Herbart was primarily concerned with the second element, instruction; and it was his method of instruction which he based upon "apperception."

Herbart's method rested firmly on a theory of learning which grew out of association psychology. According to his theory, the student does more than merely perceive an object, he apperceives it as well. Apperceiving means that a student not only has a concept of a given object, but has that concept in relation to other concepts already stored in his mind because of his environment and previous conditioning.

Essentially this means that the first presentation made to a human being was not recognized as such, but was made part of the unconscious mind. Later, the second presentation recalled the former one and interacted with it. These two concepts then became the beginning of an "apperceptive mass," which, for all practical purposes, is the human mind.

Interest then becomes self-activity which, for Herbart, is the most powerful force in education, since the ideas the pupil possesses are reproduced and united with new presentations.

It was to support his framework of thinking in terms of apperception that Herbart devised a four-step method of teaching which he described in his *Outlines of Educational Doctrine* (1835).

> In teaching we need to have (1) *clearness* in the presentation of specific facts, or the elements of what is to be enacted; (2) *association* of these facts with one another and with other related facts formerly acquired is the next step in order that assimilation or apperception may

be adequately completed; (3) when sufficient facts have been clearly presented and sufficiently assimilated, they must be *systematically ordered* so that our knowledge will be more perfectly unified than it would be, did we stop short of thorough classification; (4) finally, the facts, rules, principles and classifications thus far assumed must be secured for all time by their efficient *methodical application* in exercises that call forth the vigorous self-activity of the pupil.[1]

Once his method was formulated, Herbart then founded a pedagogical seminary and practical school at the University of Konigsberg, Germany, around 1810. This was one of the first real attempts at scientific study and experimentation in education. Herbart directly supervised and criticized the students who taught in the practice school.

After twenty-five years of teaching at Konigsberg, Herbart then accepted a professorship at Gottingen. Here he spent the remainder of his years lecturing and writing about his pedagogical principles and method.

It was Herbart's followers, however, who recast these four steps into a five-part method for modern classroom teaching. They also promoted Herbartian teaching and extended the influence of his method to this country. The movement actually reached the United States late in the nineteenth century when a group of American professors from Illinois State Normal School went to Germany to study and brought back the new science of education.

In 1892, the National Herbartian Society was organized to extend further the scope of Herbart's principles and to adapt them to American conditions. This association published translations of Herbart and various German Herbartians and issued several yearbooks. As a result of this

---

[1] Johann Friedrich Herbart, *Outlines of Educational Doctrine*, trans. Alexis F. Lange, annotated by Charles DeGarmo (New York: Macmillan, 1904), pp. 53-54.

activity, most of the normal schools, which were the predominant teacher-training institutions of the early twentieth
century, were won over to the Herbartian principles and
methods. The teachers, whom the schools eventually sent to
every section of the country, greatly affected the practices of
many of our schools.

Whereas Herbart originally recommended *clearness, association, systematization,* and *methodical application* as his
method of teaching, the procedure which has evolved into
modern educational practice as the Herbartian method embraces *preparation, presentation, association, generalization,*
and *application.*

1. *Preparation,* the first of these, is based on the ancient
psychological principle of proceeding from the known to
the unknown. The teacher is rseponsible for reviving in the
student's consciousness related ideas from past experiences.
Hopefully this will arouse the pupil's interest and prepare
him for understanding of the new material. Once this is
accomplished and the learners are in a proper and receptive
frame of mind, the lesson can proceed.

2. *Presentation* is the setting forth of the material in a
concrete manner, unless there has been a previous sensory
experience. In this step, the material is examined by means
of examples, cases, and illustrations, such as readings, pictures or excursions.

3. *Association,* sometimes called "comparison" or "ab-
straction," is probably the most important of all of the five
steps. In this phase, the teacher leads the pupils by analysis
and comparison to distinguish the aspects of similarity from
the points of differentiation in the new and the old learnings. The more carefully the teacher knits the new into the
old, the more clearly is the apperceptive nature of the process
achieved.

4. *Generalization*—after the specifics are compared and
the elements of likeness abstracted, general rules or princi-

ples are formed from the previously analyzed sensory experiences. This phase is sometimes called systematization because it is here that laws and concepts are stated and refined.

5. *Application* is the final step. The teacher tries to get the students to put the generalized principles to work, sometimes by merely directing the pupils to do a specific assignment or written exercise. In this way, the teacher can determine whether the impression is sufficiently applied because this problem must be solved by each pupil individually according to the rule which was developed in the preceding step.

As a footnote to this final phase, it should be emphasized that "application" means all forms of genuine review, but not examination. The two are radically different since a review has nothing to do with praise or censure. Review is simply the repetition of several ideas, an intensifying of these ideas. Examinations, on the other hand, attempt to test the students and often prevent them from freely expressing themselves.

In order to illustrate the five steps outlined above, we might construct a geometry lesson concerning isosceles triangles according to the Herbartian method.

1. *Preparation*: Review the axioms and postulates referring to the principle of equality.

2. *Presentation*: Define and illustrate an isosceles triangle (a triangle in which two sides are equal).

3. *Association*: Show that the previously learned concepts of equality apply directly to the two sides of the isosceles triangle.

4. *Generalization*: Show that *all* isosceles triangles have two equal sides. The teacher should present many examples of isosceles triangles—ranging from geometric blocks, dress patterns and gardens to wall pennants.

5. *Application*: Assign problems involving the principle of the equality of the two sides of isosceles triangles. For example, if the sum of the sides of an isosceles triangle is 5″

and one of the equal sides is 2″, how long is each of the other sides?

In this manner, practical lessons may be devised not only for mathematics, but also for physics, chemistry, astronomy, languages, literature, theology, philosophy, and any other subjects that lead to the development of laws, rules, definitions, principles, or generalizations.

SUMMARY

The method of instruction that Johann Friedrich Herbart originated can most certainly be used on occasion by any teacher in any modern classroom. This method has many distinct advantages, including the necessity of preparation on the part of the teacher. According to this method, the teacher must have a specific aim and goal for each lesson—and this is one of the suggestions which was set forth in Chapter One as essential to a good teaching experience.

All great teachers have recognized that teaching is an art, that the success or failure of any method depends in great measure on the personal qualities of the teacher. Herbart, and especially his followers, attempted to make teaching into a science based on a mechanistic psychology which denied the spiritual nature of the soul. For Herbartians the mind functions like a material machine, and education is the attaining of knowledge. They would cry out with Francis Bacon, "Knowledge is power."

It should also be stated that Herbart was vitally concerned with motivation or interest. His contention was, however, that one did *not* need to motivate *for* the lesson, but rather that interest should be the *result* of the lesson. One of his assumptions was that there is an incipient interest in the pupil, and a well-taught lesson reenforces this and produces more interest as well. Herbart referred to this as a "many-sided" interest.

Nevertheless, the Herbartian method is not a cure-all in modern methodology; it should be used only where the subject matter lends itself to this type of treatment. As in all teaching procedures, this five-step method should be utilized only when it is best suited for the students. The teacher should take advantage of the pupils' past experiences and be certain that the rule being taught is worth teaching.

14. THE PROBLEM METHOD

*As for methods, the prime need of every person
is the capacity to think.* DEWEY

While previous chapters have focused on educational methods originated by men of other lands, there have also been significant American influences distinctly aligned to the phenomenal development of schooling in the United States. The promotion of free democratic schooling is foremost among these elements affecting American teaching practices.

Horace Mann (1796-1859) is credited with popularizing the American system of free public education for all. While secretary of the Massachusetts Board of Education in the late 1830's, Mann succeeded in convincing many reluctant people that they should pay "for the education of other men's children" for the good of society. Arguing that schooling would eliminate delinquency and crime, he said that the taxpayers ultimately would save money because they would not have to build any more prisons. Although this sanguine hope has been proven fallacious, Mann's dream of universal schooling has been realized in the United States, and it is for this reason that he is rightly called the father of American education.

Nevertheless, despite Mann's initial importance, John Dewey (1859-1952) must be regarded, by friend and foe alike, as much more influential on the American schools. Born in Burlington, Vermont, in the year Mann died, Dewey went to the University of Vermont and later received his doctorate from The Johns Hopkins University in 1886.

For several years Dewey taught philosophy; he later opened an experimental laboratory school at the University of Chicago and started to apply some of his theories in this elementary school. In 1904 he joined the faculty of Columbia University, where he taught until his death.

Although his thoughts and teachings have precipitated much discussion and interpretation, Dewey's basic philosophy about education can be indicated in a few of his pithy aphorisms:

> Education is not a preparation for life; it is life.
> Education is the reconstruction of experience.
> Education is an ongoing process.
> Education is a matter of teaching students, not subjects.

Fundamentally, Dewey's contention is that a child must be placed in simplified circumstances which require him to come face to face with the actual value of the subjects he studies. If anyone expects a child to do constructive and critical thinking when he is an adult, then the child must have received similar experiences when young. In *Democracy and Education*, Dewey wrote:

> The first office of the social organ we call the school is to provide a simplified environment. . . . As a society becomes more enlightened, it realizes that it is responsible not to transmit and conserve the whole of its existing achievements, but only such as make for a better future society.[1]

There must always be some harmony and close coordination between theory and practice. In the usual classroom the

[1] John Dewey, *Democracy and Education* (New York: Macmillan, 1916), p. 24.

students sit together but they are isolated from one another except for their common attention to the teacher. John Dewey objected to this strenuously and wrote that man is a social animal. This is usually confined to politics but Dewey contended that man's sociality lay in education.

One of the essential elements of the progressive education advocated by Dewey is learning by doing, which he insisted was the real way learning occurs. As a result of this approach, Dewey has been regarded by most of his critics as an experimental pragmatist, an instrumentalist.

It is precisely this pragmatism and experimentalism—both instrumental in character—which serve as the basis for John Dewey's philosophy for school and society, democracy and education, fact and value. Dewey himself said:

> As for methods, the prime need of every person is the capacity to think; the power to see problems, to relate facts to them, to use and enjoy ideas. If a young man or woman comes from school with this power, all other things may be in time added to him. He will find himself intellectually and morally. But, in the mass of things that have to be "learned," the ability of individuals to think is submerged. In consequence, too large a part of our citizens has left our schools without power of critical discrimination, at the mercy of special propaganda and drifting from one plan and scheme to another according to the loudest clamor of the moment.[2]

Dewey took the enthusiasm of Pestalozzi and his objects of sense realism and insisted, because of his pragmatic approach, that all of the objects and materials used in work and play should be definitely used to accomplish a specific end. For John Dewey, self-activity demanded the opportunity to investigate and experiment, to try out ideas upon things.

Although a whole chapter of *Democracy and Education*

[2] John Dewey, "The Need for Orientation" in *The Forum and Century*, XCIII (1935), p. 334.

is devoted to method, the real substance of Dewey's method is found in his volume *How We Think* (1909). Indeed, the power of critical thinking was for Dewey the best methodology.

Actually it was not too many years ago that Dewey was setting forth this view to his graduate students in the philosophy of education. It is not difficult to remember the slightly bent, mustached figure sitting behind his desk and pursuing the very steps he advocated as the proper method of teaching. He would adjust his glasses and proceed in this fashion:

> We shall illustrate what has been said by a simple case. Suppose you are walking where there is no regular path. As long as everything goes smoothly, you do not have to think about your walking; your already formed habit takes care of it. Suddenly you find a ditch in your way. You think you will jump it (supposition, plan); but to make sure, you will survey it with your eyes (observation), and you find that it is pretty wide and that the bank on the other side is slippery (facts, data). You then wonder if the ditch may not be narrower somewhere else (idea), and you look up and down the stream (observation). You do not find any good place and so are thrown back upon forming a new plan. As you are casting about, you discover a log (fact again). You ask yourself whether you could not haul that to the ditch and get it across the ditch to use as a bridge (idea again). You judge that idea is worth trying, and so you get the log and manage to put it in place and walk across (test and confirmation by overt action).[3]

Most interpreters of John Dewey have found in his voluminous and frequently ambiguous writings that one of his main goals was to establish a series of five steps as a procedure for thinking. These same steps also constituted his method of teaching.

[3] John Dewey, *How We Think* (Boston: D. C. Heath and Company, 1933), p. 105.

Termed the "problem-solving" approach to learning, these five steps require a student to: (1) recognize a problem; (2) define that problem; (3) offer many possible solutions; (4) test these hypotheses; and (5) verify the final conclusion.

Although many writers have attempted to liken the five steps of Dewey to the five steps of Herbart, a close comparison reveals that fundamentally the methods of both men have more differences than similarities. The following analysis of the problem-solving technique will illustrate this point.

1. *Recognition of a difficulty.* This sensing of a problem is sometimes also called the "felt need" for the individual learner. It is at this time that the student realizes he lacks certain knowledge and consequently feels a need to learn some principle or fact. It was Dewey's contention that if the child was not interested and did not sense the difficulty himself, he could never be made to understand anything. This is the reason why Dewey despised anything that was drilled into a child. He claimed that nothing alien should be imposed on the learner—interests should be awakened from within.

The teacher therefore creates an atmosphere of freedom, encouraging the students to present their own problems and to manifest their interests and needs rather than follow an established curriculum. Careful direction is given by the teacher to help the students to select a problem that will challenge them and at the same time suit their experience.

2. *Definition of the problem.* The student must now examine the situation thoroughly and objectively to locate the precise nature of the difficulty. Careful definition of the exact goal desired often eliminates aimless guessing and random answers. A practical illustration might be seen in the car that stops suddenly on a highway. A difficulty is immediately felt, but the motorist is unable to take action until he ascertains whether a lack of gas, a flat tire, or a mechanical failure is the problem.

ready to state a problem in meaningful terms. The teacher once again has to guide the students to a rejection of irrelevant facts and values, and then has to assist them in finding pertinent information that will help them comprehend the problem.

3. *Suggestion of possible solutions.* The naming of solutions requires the student to survey and analyze all the data available and then guess or "hypothesize" possible answers. This hypothecation takes the form of an "If . . . , then . . ." expression of relationship in the hope of deducing statements which lead to the truth. The possibility of reaching a satisfactory answer depends, in most cases, on the number of possible solutions formulated. The stories of important inventions and scientific achievements are usually records of protracted but fruitless thought until some novel suggestion adds a new element for investigation and thus makes possible a sound conclusion.

4. *Examination of hypotheses.* This step aims to eliminate poor solutions. Through it, the student tries to select the best possible solution from those advanced in the previous step. It is most important to evaluate all the facts supporting each proposal and to estimate their utility on the basis of present need. The thoroughness and soundness of this step determine, to a large degree, not only the quality of the conclusion, but also the value of the activity in organizing knowledge for later recall and application. Care must therefore be taken to avoid blanket acceptance of the first plausible solution when further investigation remains to be done.

5. *Verification of conclusions.* After the student has selected what seems to be the best proposal for a solution, it is put to the test of experience. Open-mindedness is encouraged at this point and free discussion among teacher and students must take place at this stage. What one student fails to notice, another may present to the class and, in this

solution is presented. At this stage the solution is accepted or rejected.

Naturally verification becomes the most crucial phase because, if the conclusion is not verified, then the problem has not been accurately solved and complete revision of the previous steps is required. In the case of practical problems, the verification may be a speedy and simple matter; either the proposed solution will work or it will not. However, many of the problems encountered in a course of study will be of a kind in which verification must be logical rather than experimental.

In planning to stimulate learning through the problem-solving method, there are numerous devices that may be used to create interest and encourage thinking in the desired direction.

Step 1. A bulletin board display, the showing of a motion picture, and a classroom discussion are all excellent starting points in stimulating in students a felt need for further learning. For example, a health chart on the uses of salt may easily prompt children to wonder what kind of substance salt is. Once the question is posed, the difficulty has been recognized.

Step 2. Now the children must specifically define and phrase their exact problem. They do not wish to know where to buy salt, or what salt can do as a preservative, seasoning, or melting agent, but they ask precisely, "What is salt?"

Step 3. To one student, salt may be grains of sand. Another may assert that it is not sand but some other single element, like sodium, while someone else may conjecture that salt is a combination of sodium and chlorine.

Step 4. Each of the previous suggestions is now tested. Since spinach grows in sand, one might attempt to grow spinach in salt to see if the results are the same; this test will show, however, that spinach does not grow in salt, so salt is not the same as sand particles. Plain sodium is not the same as salt, so only the last solution remains—salt must be a combination of sodium and chlorine.

Step 5. To verify the above conclusion, the teacher adds sodium to chlorine. The result is salt and the students have learned that salt is a chemical combination of two elements, sodium and chlorine.

This process of problem-solving, while usually aiming at a single needed item of knowledge, at the same time gives vitality and value to a number of other items. The reason for this lies in the nature of the process itself, insofar as the solution of a problem requires a review of all available information having apparent bearing on the matter. In this way, many facts that would otherwise have been retained only for a brief period are brought sharply into consciousness for a new evaluation and are given associations and connections of the most desirable sort.

Consequently, teachers have attempted to use the problem-solving method in every grade and with every subject. Such practitioners have erroneously concluded that learning by doing is the only way a child can learn. Obviously a brief glance at the principles and procedures set forth in previous chapters underlines the severe inadequacy of such a limited approach to teaching.

SUMMARY

The solving of problems as advocated by John Dewey comprises an important phase of methodology in the field of teaching as well as an intrinsic aspect of daily life. While its chief advantage lies in providing students with training in reasoning, this procedure also helps learners to avoid hasty conclusions, to weigh different possible solutions, and to suspend judgment until there is sufficient evidence to come to a valid conclusion.

Nevertheless, the limitations in this progressive approach to education cannot go unmentioned. It must be remembered that, in *Democracy and Education,* Dewey assumed a naturalistic account of man, "Since growth is the characteristic of life, education is all one with growing; it has no end beyond itself."[4] This naturalism is currently the assumption of the official aim of learning in American schools. Man is considered to be naturally good, as Rousseau suggested, being liable to evil only if affected by bad social arrangements, which is a denial of original sin and its effects.

The American Constitution, for example, was written from the opposite assumption: It has a realistic conception of man—potentially good, but also potentially a beast. Hence no power was granted without checks. America is now popularly thought to be ruled by the will of the majority. It is, of course, no such thing, for that state of affairs leads to tyranny. America is under the rule of the majority, tempered by justice. Constitutionalism, not universal rule, came first.

The popular notion of liberty in the schools is the absence of all restraint. But, as the Harvard Report of 1945 states, freedom is submission to the best and fullest truth that can be known; yet it is also a recognition that truth is not fully known.

Another feature of the philosophy and psychology of John Dewey is his rejection of the notion of the dual nature of man. Since Dewey does not admit the existence of an immaterial, spiritual soul, the method of teaching which he advocates does not take this aspect of man into consideration.

In fairness to Dewey's method, however, it must be said that teachers should recognize and invoke the interests of

---

[4] *Democracy and Education, op. cit.,* p. 62.

the child, as he recommends, because much of the child's learning is dependent on strong motivation.

In conclusion, it is not unrealistic to admit that much learning is indeed learning by doing, although advocates of progressive education (a much inflated and amorphous term) attempt to have one think that it is the only way we learn. To believe that knowledge is gained only in this manner is educational fallacy.

15. THE PROJECT METHOD

*A problem must be placed in a natural setting
to be truly educational.* KILPATRICK

"Imagine a girl—her mother away—who sets out to get dinner for the family and a guest that her father is bringing home with him. She has for some time been wishing for a chance to prepare and serve, 'all by herself,' a more elaborate dinner than the family usually has. . . . So far we have the first step, purposing: the girl purposes to serve a good dinner. It seems too to be a whole-hearted purpose.

"With this purpose in mind, she plans her meal: what the menu shall be, how she will set and dress the table, and how she will serve the meal. Her course in home economics at school makes her feel surer of herself. . . . So this is the second step, planning: she plans in advance all that she will do.

"Then follows the third step, the executing. Some last-minute things must be ordered from the grocer. . . . Everything must be prepared, cooked and finally served, the table meanwhile having been made ready. In this case the executing extends to the end of the meal and even afterwards. . . .

"Last comes judging. How well did she succeed? . . . She tries to appraise it all fairly, for she means to succeed as a housekeeper. So she asks of each thing, 'Did I do what I planned? How well did I succeed?' . . . If she really means to profit best by her experience, she will ask further, 'Now that it is all over, what have I learned? What mistakes did I make? Wherein could I do better next time?"[1]

In the preceding explanation, Professor William Heard Kilpatrick (1871-1965) set forth the four basic steps necessary to the successful performance of his technique of teaching known as the project method.

Basically, Kilpatrick considered the project as an adaptation of Dewey's problem method. Kilpatrick emphasized the progressive approach to teaching and then tried to apply it to the traditional curriculum. Previous endeavors to apply problem-solving to American schools had frequently deteriorated into mere formalism because of the failure to modernize the teacher-centered course of study. Even as educators attempted revision, there was a similar need for a flexible method to accompany the growth of democratic education.

Kilpatrick did not regard his proposals as unique; rather he preferred to think of himself as Dewey's interpreter. He presented the project not as a startling innovation, but as an attempt to restore progressivism to its former pristine place of honor in the schools conducted by the instrumentalists and the pragmatists.

It is indeed true that Kilpatrick did not offer anything new. In essence he advocated the use of purposeful activity, a project, as a learning experience for students. Although not stated in the same way previously, such projects have been used down through the centuries.

One of the many precedents that can be cited for the use of projects as a teaching device, is their use at Eton, the English preparatory school. Ever since its establishment as the King's College of Our Lady of Eton beside Windsor in 1440, this famous public school has assigned to its students certain chores and duties designed to teach as well

---

[1] William Heard Kilpatrick, *Foundations of Method* (New York: The Macmillan Company, 1930), pp. 204-205.

as to train them. This is especially true in the field of
agriculture. The cultivation of a small section of the land
immediately adjacent to the buildings has been a part of
the daily curriculum down through the years. These assignments or projects have been carried out not merely for
the food they produced, but also for the training they provided to the students. To this day, the Etonians, though
wearing formal attire to class, perform projects in their shop
periods.

Going back to a still earlier period in the history of
education, the monastic schools also based much of their
operation on the project principle. As a matter of historical
fact, St. Benedict (?480-543) founded his monastery at Monte
Cassino in 529 with the motto, *Ora et Labora*. His famous
Benedictine Rule did much to preserve learning during
the so-called Dark Ages by maintaining the necessary balance and moderation between the prayer life and the work
life of study and farming.

Particularly akin to the project approach of today was
the copying of valuable manuscripts and the practice of
assigning to each monk a specific plot of ground for cultivation. The monk in turn would teach the basic skills to the
neighboring farmers whose lands had been ravished by the
Barbarian invaders.

In the middle of the last century in the United States,
a number of schools or colleges of agriculture were founded
to teach young men the new techniques for milking, grazing,
planting, and so on. Projects for these students were the
application of the principles learned at school on their
families' farms.

All these examples require a definite purpose and the
application of some principle—whether transcribing, raking,
cultivating, or using a lathe—in a natural setting. It is in
precisely this respect that Kilpatrick endeavored to use his
project approach to teaching. He proposed the use of problem solving in a natural setting so that the student would

learn to appraise his conditions, conceive a plan for solution, set up ways and means of fulfilling his plan, and finally check his results. The final achievement would not only be the realization of a tangible project but, most importantly, the acquisition of considerable knowledge by the learner. This project learning, according to Kilpatrick, could be classified into four different types, each distinguished by a particular purpose:

> Type I is the Producer's Project, in which the purpose is to produce something. This varies through the widest conceivable range in importance, from the smallest child's most temporary sand house to the making of a nation or a world association of nations—in material that may be used, from the stone in the walk under our feet to the spiritual yearning of a prayer. Wherever there is activity dominated by the purpose to produce, there we have a project of Type I.

> . . . The next is Type II, the Consumer's Project. In this the purpose is to consume, to use in some way, to use and enjoy. A small boy has the opportunity to see fireworks. His purpose makes his eyes follow the rockets high into the air, as he looks eagerly to see the bomb burst. The boy is, as regards production, merely passive; but he is very active in consuming, taking in, enjoying what some one else has produced. An artist paints a picture, a producer's project. I and others come to see and enjoy, a consumer's project. . . .

> . . . Type III is the Problem Project, where the purpose is to solve a problem, to clear up some intellectual difficulty. Historically and individually this is probably to be thought of as an outgrowth of Type I. Almost any purpose to produce, especially if it be educative, will involve some difficulty which in turn will call for thinking.[1]

> Type IV . . . is sometimes called the Drill Project, though I prefer to call it the Specific Learning Project.

[1] *Ibid.*, pp. 347-348.

In it the purpose is to acquire some item or degree of skill or knowledge . . . for example, to attain a certain speed and accuracy in column addition.[2]

In the progressive tradition of John Dewey, Kilpatrick stressed that all four such projects, although distinct in essential purpose, must involve the interests of the student to be successful. Once motivated, a project was for the learner "any unit of purposeful experience, any instance of purposeful activity where the dominating purpose, as an inner urge, (1) fixes the aim of the action, (2) guides its purpose, and (3) furnishes its drive, its inner motivation."[3]

Hence it is imperative in an ideal project that a student investigate an area of interest meaningful to him. Hopefully further interest in the topic will be generated and developed as the project is brought to fruition. The student is learning by doing in the true sense, and the self-activity which Dewey also advocated is also assured.

How, then, does Kilpatrick's project method differ from Dewey's problem-solving approach? Basically, the project is a refined version of the problem. While the problem requires the formulation and testing of various definite hypotheses, the project seeks to emphasize only one approach to a particular area of interest. As soon as the student selects this area, he works to illustrate and illuminate this topic in a meaningful manner. Data will be evaluated and eliminated in the process, but just insofar as they clarify the topic.

Only one solution is worked out and nothing has to be affirmed or denied in the project approach. The student merely sets out to prove or confirm some specific area which he desires to know more about.

While the problem seeks to produce an answer to a

[2] *Ibid.*, p. 355.

[3] William Heard Kilpatrick, "Dangers and Difficulties of the Project Method and How to Overcome Them," *Teachers College Record*, XXII, September, 1926, p. 183.

specific question about which no conclusions have been ascertained, the project often requires previous familiarity with the main aspects of the topic. For this reason, projects can serve equally well as initiating and culminating activities.

Furthermore, since emotions and feelings are part and parcel of "the whole child," Kilpatrick insisted that the project method was more effective than Dewey's problem method, which mainly stressed the cognitive powers. In his *Foundations of Method,* Kilpatrick elaborated on the esthetic importance of his method. He advocated that the teacher communicate the basic value of appreciation by revealing his own feelings to the children who will then catch on by a sort of contagion. An effective way of spreading this contagion, Kilpatrick suggested, is to allow the students to become productive by painting, dancing, dramatizing, and other creative exercises.

The young girl preparing her family's meal certainly produced many manifestations of her abilities—a tempting casserole, an exotic salad, or perhaps a delicate frappe. All were separate projects that had a definite purpose (to delight the family and the guest) and all were planned, executed, and evaluated with great care by the enthusiastic young cook.

She certainly had received previous training and advice and followed certain recipes, but she produced the actual project herself. As with any project, the ultimate success in this case depended on the creative enterprise and ingenuity of the individual worker.

Have you ever made a pin-hole camera, a miniature Roman battle array, or a soap model of an Elizabethan theater? If not, surely at one time in your educational experience, you have been assigned a term paper or a special report. Whether you realized it at the time or not, you were not only acquiring meaningful information, but you were also engaging in the execution of a project. The production of this chapter, and indeed this whole volume, is a definite project for the author. If you are reading this with the purpose of learning how to be a better teacher, then you too are now participating in a project.

As typified by the four types of projects (producer's, consumer's, problem, and drill) outlined by Kilpatrick, such activities take many forms. The specific purpose of each product determines whether the product will be a manual creation, an esthetic enjoyment, an intellectual concept, an appreciation, an attitude, or a basic skill.

Too often students engage in a project without realizing that a definite purpose should exist. This distortion of the method results in the mere performance of a task. If a student undertakes the writing of a term report merely as an assignment for credit, then he misses the whole merit of the project. The research, assimilation, and compilation of new data will become no more than drudgery or busywork. His aim, in such a case, will be to get it finished rather than to enjoy and appreciate the learnings he is experiencing. Likewise, if a student builds a model theater or fortress but does not grasp the historical facts and concepts that created it, then his activity is simply play construction. In both these instances, an essential learning purpose was missing. Such attempts at projects, which are arbitrarily assigned, usually fail to provoke the genuine motivating interest of the student as well. Essentially, then, such tasks are not projects because they do not center on the learner's desires, needs, and purposes.

A good project, therefore, should not be imposed, but should arise, in the progressive tradition, out of the interests of the child. A general area or topic of the curriculum—historical invention, animal life, modern automation, or new nations—can be suggested by the teacher, but from this general recommendation the child should be free to choose the phase of activity he wishes to explore. The student should also be allowed to determine, in accordance with his special talents and inclinations, the manner of the project's expression—report, dramatization, model, diorama, poster, collection, scrapbook, miniature figures.

The teacher serves as a guide, checking that the project will consist of real learning activities in general harmony with the current course of study. This is necessary to prevent confusion and misinterpretation of broad themes. By indirect yet enthusiastic leadership, the teacher also watches the progress of each student in order to insure that pertinent and valuable facts, principles, and skills are mastered—in correspondence to individual ability.

The students should be made conscious that their projects present an opportunity for many new learnings; they should also be encouraged to consult as many sources as possible to achieve their goals. Students and teacher alike should be equally cognizant of the four phases or steps which Kilpatrick formulated for a successful project:

1. *Purposing.* Just as the young girl described by Kilpatrick determined that her purpose was the serving of a good dinner, so also an individual student must set a definite purpose before embarking on his project. In a biology class, a student might intend to produce a study of the human heart, while in an art class the purposes of a particular pupil might be to examine carefully the works of Renoir and compare them in contrast, line, and symbolism to the paintings of a contemporary artist.

2. *Planning.* Complete and comprehensive planning is as essential to a school project as it was to the girl's dinner. For biology and art students, books, representations, and illustrations about their topics must be thoroughly perused and pondered and the most apt application must be envisioned for presentation. If an outline or plan is not made,

the results may be handicapped by irrelevant as well as helter-skelter work. In this step also, the student, while consulting many books, periodicals, resource persons, and institutions of enrichment, will have the opportunity to develop new skills and interests that are a guide to further learning.

3. *Executing.* The height of interest in the project should be aroused in the student at the point when he puts his plans into action. Serving the dinner must have been the proudest moment for Kilpatrick's young girl, much the same as constructing a model heart would give crowning satisfaction to a biology student. A folio of artistic pieces and a scholarly paper on the results of the comparisons made by the art student would likewise be a source of accomplishment.

4. *Judging.* The final step requires that the students evaluate the success of the project in relation to the original purpose. Appraisal of new learnings and skills is also important in examining the overall worth of the activity. Was the effort worth the knowledge gained, and was the organizational approach conducive to effective learning outcomes? These and other questions should be asked by the teacher and student to determine the extent of both success and failure, with a view to further improvement and proficiency in future projects.

In recalling the four types of projects defined by Kilpatrick, it is evident that the above framework pertains equally to (1) physical products or material projects, (2) simple learning or appreciation projects, (3) problem or intellectual projects, and (4) specific purpose or skill projects. Consequently, many aspects of the curriculum—social studies, science and mathematics, philosophy, art, literature —offer boundless opportunities throughout the grades and at higher levels for learning by the project method.

SUMMARY

Accentuating demands for the practical and the demonstrable, William Heard Kilpatrick's project method has been hailed by many educators as the saving gesture in the progressive movement. While it is true that project teaching has provided a flexible and practical new emphasis to individual learning by doing, caution must be exercised.

For instance, it is only natural that when a student chooses a project he wants to present his best work. As a result, competition will oftentimes lead to misplaced emphasis on elaborate construction and expensive materials as well as over-zealous parental assistance, rather than individual learning benefit. Practices of this sort become notorious at the popular-science fairs or open school exhibits, where everyone comes to see what John and Mary have been doing in school.

Herein lies the most serious limitation to the project method—the real learning purpose frequently becomes subordinated to the desire to surpass other students. It is therefore the teacher's primary duty to motivate and inspire confidence in the students as individual workers. The interest of the pupils in the learning goal itself—not the exterior presentation—must remain foremost.

The teacher must also recognize that the class schedule cannot be one continuous flow of projects. Much explanation and other training are necessary in the curriculum to provide the foundations for worthwhile projects and to prevent gaps in learning.

There must also be a conscious effort to develop in the students such qualities as originality and cooperation; the ability to follow as well as to lead; the habits of persistence in challenging work and acceptance of responsibility; and the proper appreciation of the opportunities offered by society. These skills and attitudes are essential to the progress of the student, and in fact mastery of these qualities as well as specific content knowledge is more important than the actual project in final evaluation. It is for this reason that poor workmanship will generally be praised as much as a handsome job. Each project must be judged on its own merits and on the growth of the student, not in comparison to other students' work. This presents a somewhat arbitrary standard, and impartiality on the teacher's part becomes vital.

Teachers, students, and parents also must be fully aware that the project is primarily an individual experience. Success is measured by personal growth in accordance with the aims of the person engaged in the activity. As a method of teaching and learning, the project therefore has a potential as great as the sincerity and conscientious effort of the individual student. To the teacher belong the roles of leader, chairman, coach, umpire, taskmaster, adviser, examiner, guide, or sympathetic listener, as the occasion may require.

16. THE UNIT METHOD

Herbart's steps are renamed and combined in a single lesson plan.

"In unity there is strength" is a maxim known to almost every school child. Although this Revolutionary War cry was used as a rallying force to join the thirteen colonies into an independent nation, such a motto might also have been adopted during the early 1920's in support of a new concept in teaching.

The goal of unit teaching, as championed at the University of Chicago, by Professor Henry C. Morrison (1871-1945), was sought as a reaction to the free-wheeling and often exaggerated use of self-activity that was producing helter-skelter learning in many progressive classrooms. Among Morrison's followers were William C. Bagley of Teachers' College, Columbia University, and Ross L. Finney of the University of Minnesota.

Recalling that the term "unity" implied oneness, completeness, harmony, and solidarity to our colonial forefathers these three educators proposed that a "unit" of school activity would likewise provide students with the opportunity for full and thorough learning experiences.

In criticizing the excessive emphasis on students' "felt needs" and particular interests as manifested in problem-solving and project work, Morrison and his associates also rejected that most prominent alternative technique which required memorizing and reciting isolated facts. These men, classified as essentialists, were convinced that it was far more valuable for the curriculum to include a certain fundamental body of knowledge rather than to rely on disjointed spurts of pupil interest or memorized lesson fragments. In order to unify and transmit this essential core of knowledge, deemed necessary for a well-rounded education, Morrison devised the unit method of teaching.

The philosophy underlying this approach is that certain essential material can and should be taught in a unified pattern which is determined by the judgment of the teacher, not by the choice of the students. It is also the responsibility of the teacher, however, to present the material in such a way that the students will soon be motivated and desire to explore the topic fully. In other words, the interest of the child is still very important, but the teacher does not have to wait for it to come from within the child as in the Dewey-Kilpatrick tradition. This goal is achieved by the teacher through a unity of purpose, plan, and method.

Unity of purpose involves a recognition of the essential harmony or solidarity of the curriculum. In social studies alone, the student must be aware of his neighborhood, community, state, country, and world. Each area must be studied in sequential fashion to insure a meaningful understanding of the privileges and obligations of living in America.

Unity of plan requires the teacher to focus on a topic about to be considered before the students are introduced to it. Here the teacher must attempt to foresee all the area subdivisions, objectives, and potential activities that will be necessary to develop the general theme fully. Tests must be prepared at this time and relevant resource materials should be investigated and enlisted. Stimulating motivations to launch the approaching unit successfully must also be outlined. An actual written plan must be drawn up to include all these factors. Morrison termed such a unit plan, which replaced many single, disjointed lesson plans, "mastery teaching."

Unity of method is achieved by practicing the unique five-step procedure designed by Morrison to transmit a unit of new learning. As suggested in his *Practice of Teaching in the Secondary School,* the method can be described as "pretest, teach, test the result, adapt procedure, teach and test again to the point of actual learning."

Morrison's five steps were similar to a five-step stairway. The bottom landing where the student stands marks the last unit of knowledge he has mastered. Now ready to attempt to reach the next landing which represents new learning, he must first climb five steps. In many cases, two or three steps might be visualized as higher or wider than the others and requiring a longer time to ascend. The rate of progress depends on the difficulty of the material and the child's ability to master it. Consequently, some units may last one or two weeks and some may extend into month-long periods. Whatever the length of time, however, by the end of the unit the student should have thoroughly mastered a unified body of knowledge pertaining to a certain essential topic. He is also now prepared to scale a new stairway.

In general, Morrison designed the unit method to involve an entire class of students, with allowances made during the development of the unit for individual capacities and varied interests. Gradually, however, as the unit method was accepted throughout the country, minor variations of approach were practiced. A teacher in Dalton, Massachusetts, Helen H. Parkhurst, geared the units for individual students to execute. In order to insure that each student would carry through all the phases of activity necessary for a complete mastery of the topic, a contract explicitly agreeing to the requirements would be signed by teacher and student before the unit was undertaken. The student would then proceed at his own speed and ability, with the teacher acting as a guide to ascertain that the five steps were properly carried out. Known as the Dalton Plan or Contract Plan of teaching, this method naturally requires greater work on the teacher's part in planning and directing many units at a time.

Still another modification of unit activity was originated in the Winnetka, Illinois, schools. Appropriately labeled the "Winnetka Plan," this procedure also called for a unit of work—but as a group effort, not on an individual basis. In this manner, three or four units proceeded at the same time, each providing opportunities to share and compromise, to lead, and follow. In general, the teacher would make certain that the unit of work was divided proportionately and according to each student's potential. This was accomplished by administering a diagnostic test to the children at the beginning of the unit in order to determine what goals and tasks each should undertake. Later, when each child thought he had achieved his own goals, he took a self-administered test to see if he was ready for testing by the teacher and able to advance to new learning tasks.

Despite the minor variations in unit teaching that have been advocated by proponents of the Dalton and Winnetka Plans, Morrison's fundamental method remains the same. Whether it is for an individual, a group, or a whole class, the unit consists basically of replacing daily lessons and disjointed projects with the mastery teaching of a well planned, unified, and essential body of knowledge divided into a system of five steps.

1. *Exploration*. This is a warm-up period during which the teacher questions, discusses, and tests the pupils to determine how much they already know about a proposed unit.

2. *Presentation*. Once the teacher has decided which phases of the unit need the most emphasis, he now uses a lecture or demonstration giving an overview of the unit. This initial phase of presentation is geared toward stimulating the children's interest so that they will be eager to

proceed. On subsequent days the teacher will continue to sustain interest with further presentation and development of the material. (This reverts to the Herbartian idea of creating interest, rather than Dewey's philosophy of exclusively following the interest of the pupil.) After the teacher feels that the presentation of the topic has been completed, he tests the students to check which points need clarification or amplification.

3. *Assimilation.* This consists mainly in a revised presentation adapted to the students' capacities as manifested on the test. Other sources are also pointed out by the teacher, so that the students can come to a fuller understanding of the unit. Resource persons, field trips, films, or other enrichments are provided as the opportunity warrants. Once again the teacher tests the results after this phase of activity.

4. *Organization.* As a basically child-centered form of activity, this step requires the students to come to conclusions about the material presented in the unit. Through a report, a project, a dramatization, a panel or various other activities, the students are responsible for organizing the new learnings into some logical form of digest or interpretation.

5. *Recitation.* After the formal organization of the material, the students are then expected to present clearly the final results of their work, either orally or in writing.

A model unit will now be outlined for purposes of practical illustration. The social studies area has been selected and the topic has been narrowed down to a unit on local town history. The setting is a fourth grade classroom in a modern school at Syosset, New York, a small town on Long Island.

Before the unit can be launched, the teacher must prepare an appropriate plan.

Overview. This unit is designed to acquaint the students with the highlights of Syosset's local history. A general, factual, educational, cultural, and social picture will be drawn. While today the town is a modern residential area, only fifty years ago it was farmland and had only one general store.

Objectives

A. General

1. to give the students a deeper appreciation of the significant history of Syosset;

2. to broaden the students' understanding of the early settlers' occupations contrasted with today's modern environment;

3. to stimulate an attitude of pride in all current community facilities by picturing Syosset without such vital necessities as water, gas, lights, and transportation;

4. to give the children a personal view of the people and their activities, especially chores, games, and sports, with particular emphasis on school life, in early Syosset.

B. Specific

1. to point out individual landmarks and turning points;

2. to stress certain dates and significant locations of old farms and landmarks, especially in relation to familiar structures;

3. to take each community service individually and outline its development;

4. to single out particular personalities of lasting greatness;

5. to develop skills of cooperative planning and responsible project accomplishment.

Pupil's General Aim: to find out about the inhabitants of this area in former years and to explore the type of surroundings the people had and to see how their culture and way of life have affected us.

Pupil's Specific Aims: to be determined on an individual basis.

Chronological Outline of major areas

1. founding by Robert Williams in 1648.

2. the Matinecock Indians.

3. settlers before 1900; importance of the Dutch.
4. the farms.
5. roads and transportation; the railroad in 1854.
6. post office.
7. fire department; organized in 1915.
8. police protection and community services.
9. bank, library.
10. the hotel.
11. general store.
12. first industry.
13. important people.
14. amusements.
15. school (special emphasis).

Proposed Activities

1. field trips to original school, bank, library, and fire department.
2. examination of a collection of newspaper articles written about Syosset history.
3. bulletin board display of old documents and pictures of original buildings and landmarks.
4. interview with old-timers and other resource persons.
5. compilation of "Syosset History Book."
6. dramatization for school assembly.

Necessary materials

1. library resources.
2. newspaper articles about Syosset; town history by Patricia Tunison.
3. numerous town records and documents.
4. interviews with old-timers in the Syosset neighborhood.
5. pictures from files of town and interested families.

The actual steps of the unit could then be carried out in this fashion:

1. *Exploration.* The teacher questions students on Syosset history—how far back they can remember, what parents and grandparents have told them, etc. Possible test to determine exact nature and depth of knowledge.

2. *Presentation.* A scrapbook showing old scenes and buildings is shown to stimulate interest and questions. In proper sequence, the areas listed in the plan are presented and explored in conformity with the enumerated aims and objectives. After several presentations of the material, a test is given.

3. *Assimilation.* The data are then recast and reemphasized according to the student needs revealed by the test. Here resource persons, field trips, and other enrichment activities can be utilized as needed. Another test will be administered.

4. *Organization.* The students will now be responsible for organizing the facts for presentation in a class history book and for a dramatization at a general school assembly.

5. *Recitation.* The finished book and performance of the play will serve as the final recitation results.

SUMMARY

Just as there is strength in unity, so also there is a tremendous amount of solid work for the teacher in unit planning. Since an incomplete or superficial unit can be more harmful than the fragmented teaching it seeks to counteract, diligent preparation and forethought are required of the teacher in all cases. A well-planned and carefully executed unit, however, cannot be exceeded in clarity and overall mastery in learning experience. Furthermore the time and effort spent in the ground work often pay off most economically for both teacher and student once the unit is launched. The direction is clear, the path has been mapped out, and there is little time for delay in unit work. Both tests and assignments have been prepared in advance, leaving the teacher free for her crucial role as guide and director.

Some of the best elements of previous methods are blended into the smooth and harmonious functioning of unit activity. There is lecturing, discussion, demonstration, show-and-tell, thoughtful questioning, problem solving, project work, and continuous evaluation.

The unit is flexible and comprehensive, lending itself to refreshing and stimulating application from kindergarten through high school and even in some college courses. Not only social studies but science, literature, art, music, health, safety, mathematics, language, and religion are equally adaptable to unit teaching. Wherever there is a basic body of knowledge to be communicated as a whole or unit, there is an opportunity to use the method of Henry C. Morrison.

17. THE SOCIALIZED
RECITATION

Let's try group participation in learning.

A few years ago headlines from London announced
that a lack of money was forcing the unique Burgess Hill
Freedom School to close. Often described as a school which
"looked like a beatnik colony," Burgess Hill was notorious
for letting its students do just what they felt like doing—
including smoking in class, swearing, drinking, necking,
or not attending sessions for weeks or years at a time. The
students at Burgess Hill had been free to speak out or express themselves in any manner they chose. Absolute license
ran rampant under the guise of freedom.

Such activity was a far cry from the days of Pythagoras
(*c.* 500 B.C.) when students were rarely permitted to speak
in the classroom. In fact the great mathematician maintained
that no pupil should be allowed to talk in class for at least
three years because it would take him that long to begin
drawing valid conclusions!

There is no doubt that both the Pythagorean theory and
the Burgess Hill code were extremes between which many
variations have developed throughout the centuries. Rousseau's theories of self-activity and free expression were modified and adapted in differing degrees by Pestalozzi, Dewey,
and Kilpatrick. In like manner, the traditional recitation

in which "the child responded only when spoken to" had also been revised and changed with the times.

Considering the term "recitation" itself, the teacher was for many centuries merely a "hearer of lessons" which he had previously cited and the pupils "re-cited" back to him. The student either went up to the teacher's desk to present his recitation or the entire class recited the required exercise in unison. Naturally this method was confined, in many instances, to a strict memorization of limited passages. Dominating the classroom in this manner, teachers were often eager to adapt the Herbartian Method since it provided a set formula for imparting a fixed curriculum.

A number of events and theories, however, combined to cause drastic changes in the American schools of the 1930's. The end of Victorian attitudes, World War I, the Great Depression, and the granting of the vote to women, along with the democratic principles of classroom management, were only a few of the many factors that served to promote an innovation in method known as the socialized recitation. Such socialism in action in American schools was indeed a product of the times, and no particular person or group can be entirely credited with the new approach to learning which evolved.

No longer was the emphasis on "re-citing." Socializing now became central in classroom practice. Just as problems and projects could be viewed as an approach to the windward side of education with stress on the child's interests, so also the socialized recitation method can be considered as the leeward approach with emphasis on the societal aspects of the classroom.

Many believed that, since man is naturally a social being, an important part of his education should concentrate on developing desirable relationships and interactions with others. In the traditional manner of recitation, a child would wait and prepare for his own turn and would rarely pay attention when others were called upon. Since few answers demanded more than a parrot-like repetition, there was seldom any refutation or amplification of what anyone else had said. The philosophy underlying the socialized recitation, however, aimed at eliciting answers based on insight and reasoning and directed toward one's peers, not to the teacher exclusively.

Socialized recitation, then, is defined as group participation in learning. Through a common exchange of ideas, members of the class are required not only to express their own ideas but also to think reflectively and to appreciate what others say in order to refute or support it as the lesson progresses. No student can remain isolated or indifferent—each must realize that he is learning not only from the teacher but from all those around him.

To understand the significance of the socialized recitation in modern schools, it is most helpful to determine exactly what is meant by both the adjective "socialized" and the noun "recitation" in the term.

"Socialized" refers in the field of education to togetherness or groupness—a "we" feeling for the classroom. For students, socialization requires a recognition of common learning goals and a desire to achieve such goals together.

"Recitation" is a form of student classroom response. It requires previous knowledge of certain content gained from actual experience, a previous lesson presented by the teacher, or reading the textbook and other supplementary materials. From these sources the student is supposed to recall certain information and offer it when called.

By socializing the recitation, the teacher expects the students to address the required response not to himself but to the whole class. Others are then encouraged to comment, amplify, or disagree with a student's answer. Naturally, isolated facts, dates, or one-word replies are not particularly conducive to stimulating insight or perceptive relationships, so the role of the teacher demands creative planning and purposeful questioning skills. The gearing of topics toward reflective thinking is consequently crucial to this method, and teachers should strive to conduct the recitation in such a manner that the students become eager to interact, discuss, analyze, and even question each other.

Essentially, then, this approach aims for a socializing rather than an individualizing of the educational experience. In stressing the democratic rather than the individual framework, "group" becomes a key word.

Considered in this aspect, the socialized recitation can take many forms or shades in practice, including the following.

1. *Change in pupil position.* This usually attempts to promote the "we" feeling by arranging the students' chairs and desks in circular or grouped arrangements. The students become more conscious of one another and are inclined automatically to formulate and direct responses to fellow students instead of to the teacher alone.

2. *Change in teacher position.* By moving his desk to the back or side of the room, the teacher consequently takes the focus of attention away from himself. Even if a student does turn to render a response in the teacher's direction, the presence of the others cannot be overlooked in such a situation.

3. *Personnel variations.* This technique would offer various students the opportunity to ask questions or initiate a discussion based on certain content the teacher had previously prescribed. The fact that a member of one's peer group is directing the activity tends to reduce tensions and encourage freer expression of ideas. It also removes the emphasis from the teacher and centers it fully on the group.

4. *Spirit of the activity.* Even when desks, chairs, students, and teacher remain in customary positions, the socialized recitation may be carried out by a simple feeling of group solidarity and interaction. A teacher may select one student at a time to respond to the whole group, or he may request

the class as a unit to discuss a topic and formulate general conclusions in much the same manner as a congress or senate would function. Dissenting views as well as majority judgments would later be presented either in oral or written form.

Most often the teacher divides the class into informal subgroups, presents a topic, problem, or question, and allows time for each subgroup to react, deliberate, and decide upon a united solution. The various subgroups then present their decisions to the whole class. In all of these situations, a spirit of unity prevails, relaxing the participants and eliciting a socialized interaction among group members. The actual means used to produce the activity of a socialized recitation may take several different forms. The most common type is a question from the teacher or another student. As stimuli to both reflective thinking and socialized response, the three most purposeful kinds of questions are:

a. *Comparison questions,* which require a student to relate or contrast various likenesses or differences of actions, policies, objects, etc. Since comparison is one of the steps in the process of reasoning, questions of this type can provide much opportunity for insight and perception.

b. *Analysis questions,* which invite the learner to investigate and break down certain principles, laws, data, or other factors in order better to recognize the pertinence of various situations.

c. *Judgment questions* are concerned with discerning relationships, or determining worth and value. All questions involving criticism are also of this type. In judgment questions, the answer must affirm or deny something because of a specific reason or conclusion.

In actual practice, there is no sharp line of division between these three broad kinds of questions. Similarly, no one type should be used exclusively because responses vary in complexity and difficulty.

In addition to various questions, many problems and

projects geared to group performance may also be suggested by the teacher as additional means of fostering the socialized recitation.

A particularly helpful common experience such as a visit from a special resource person or a worthwhile film might also evoke valuable interaction, discussion, and evaluation by the group.

The more often such a lesson permits a student to relate to others, the more socialized the recitation becomes. Generally, controversial issues in literature, politics, or economics are acutely adaptable to such an exchange in the classroom setting. Social studies, science, philosophy, mathematics, current events, and the arts are also excellent subject areas for this method. It is generally agreed that teachers in the secondary, collegiate, and graduate levels can make the best use of the socialized recitation because, by these stages of development, students should have recognized the value of thinking before they speak, and have learned to respect the rights and feelings of others.

SUMMARY

It has been said that no man is an island; no man stands alone. This is just as true in education as it is in all other aspects of our democratic society. Just as in our world men of many lands negotiate with and help one another, so also in the classroom students of different backgrounds and abilities exchange ideas and teach one another.

This is the essence of socialism in education and, in its ideal aspect, it is indeed a valuable tool. Students not only learn the importance of group learning and reflective thinking, but they also come to appreciate varied viewpoints. They recognize that different plausible conclusions can be drawn from the same data.

The socialized recitation also offers students valuable

training in the power of effective communication. These lessons also place a premium on pupil-centered participation, and initiative is inherently encouraged. In the ideal situation, there is group learning by doing in the fullest sense.

The part of the teacher, however, must not be overlooked. Although indirect, the teacher's efforts are crucial in safeguarding fundamental discipline and in preventing too frequent digressions. The teacher must also make certain that all students become involved—encouraging shy or timid learners to respond, while preventing a few from monopolizing the procedure.

For greatest success in launching and maintaining the socialized recitation, the teacher should spend considerable time planning thoughtful questions, problems, or projects for the class. Likewise both teacher and students should be adequately prepared beforehand about the topic under consideration.

Finally, although interpretations may vary, it must be stressed that the unrestrained anarchy of Burgess Hill is as undesirable as the stringent docility of Pythagorean times. The keynote of the socialized recitation should be a spirit of united and responsible cooperation. With such a concept as a goal, this method of teaching can be a valuable asset in fostering individual growth through group experience in the classroom.

18. THE MONTESSORI
METHOD

Retarded children teach us how to teach.

Let us imagine a scene which could easily have happened in 1894 when Maria Montessori became the first woman ever to receive a medical degree from the University of Rome.

"Congratulations, Maria, we are certainly proud of you," one of her friends must have said.

Maria Montessori undoubtedly voiced her "thank you" as a gesture of gratitude, and then tried to get back to her family for a reunion.

But Claudia Uccello and the others kept urging her, "Are you going into research now, Doctor Montessori? You know there will be a reaction among certain people against the ministrations of a woman."

"No, I am going ahead to be the medical doctor that I have always dreamed of becoming. Besides private practice, I am also planning to work with mentally deficient children and do further study in the psychiatric clinic."

So it can be imagined that *La Dotteressa* began the career which led to her phenomenal success in handling retarded children and her later proficiency in applying her methods to teaching normal children. By 1907 Dr. Montessori (1870-1952) was invited to organize an institution in a slum area of Rome. In that section both parents were frequently working out of the house, the older children were in school, and the little ones were left to their own devices. Maria Montessori established the *Casa Dei Bambini* to care for these youngsters. Her success with this school was so great that by 1912 her fame was worldwide and many flocked to her to learn how she did it.

Miss Montessori was humble and honest enough to admit that her theories and practices were not totally original. J. M. G. Itard (1775-1838) and Edouard Seguin (1812-1880) had done extensive work with deaf mutes and mentally defective children. Dr. Montessori utilized principles derived from their works. She also recognized her debt to David P. De Vries (1592-1655) in biology and Herbart and Friedrich Froebel (1782-1852) in education. Finally, she ascribed her success to her personal philosophy which was based on Aristotle's concept of the nature of man. She was convinced that every individual, because he is endowed with a body and an immortal soul, possesses a human dignity worthy of respect.

Dr. Montessori was therefore interested in the child's complete development as a person—physically, mentally, and spiritually. This concept determined, in large measure, her method of teaching since it is concerned with individuality and developmental readiness. This is particularly interesting since there was also a development in the methods which Montessori herself advocated. Often amazed at the interest and abilities of the three-year-olds, Montessori amplified much of her total system through observation of her charges. As she observed the little ones, methods and materials which could assist the children in learning were devised, tested, developed, and perfected.

Basically, the Montessori method consists in the utilization of the child's natural tendencies and aptitudes by means of a stimulating environment and purposeful sensory objects.

In this manner, the child in a prekindergarten or nursery situation is exposed to a variety of different teaching materials such as beads, puzzles, rods, and brightly colored numbers and letters of the alphabet in solid form. The child is free to select any object he wishes as long as he does not take more than one at a time; the teacher then explains what to do with the object (build, feel, rearrange, trace) in order that the child might learn the principle or skill the object has been designed to impart. The child is then left to practice and perfect this activity. The objects themselves are so designed to enable the students to learn the basic understandings and principles of reading, writing, arithmetic, and religion—Montessori's "4 R's."

The use of these teaching objects and tools, however, is not to be considered the total substance of the Montessori method. In fact, Montessori insisted that her approach not be so bound by specific devices that it could not be generally applied. She felt that the objects could and should be expanded and elaborated upon as experience might dictate, provided certain principles which guide the instructors are maintained.

There are five such basic and interdependent principles. The proper combination of these principles, *La Dotteressa* claimed, would result in the desired outcomes of self-mastery which she sought for young children. A brief description of her five main principles should help to explain her method.

1. *The principle of liberty.* Montessori maintained that children are not psychologically prepared to learn by the word-of-mouth methods by which adults learn. Consequently, she declared, children should be free to pass through childhood according to their own needs and within their own environments. Since this process continues independently of efforts to teach, education can only help by providing the best conditions for this experience.

Repression of spontaneous acts and the imposition of

the will of another must be avoided because such limitation prevents children from acting creatively and happily and enforces impassivity and apathy upon them.

But Dr. Montessori must not be misunderstood. The essential nature of liberty does not imply license. Liberty and law go together. For Maria Montessori, liberty and discipline are inseparable aspects of the same thing. Liberty is not the absolute freedom to do what one wishes, but only to do that which is right. Hence there are natural restrictions placed upon all children—biologically, morally, and socially.

2. *The principle of discipline.* As used in the Montessori system, this requires that the object which a child chooses can only be selected if no one else already has it. Once chosen, the object must also be used in the correct manner. Attention is thus paid to the rights of others and to the collective interest.

In this regard, all acts which are useless, dangerous, or harmful to others should be repressed, but all acts conducive to the children's freedom within proper limits should be allowed. Thus the will is trained to both activity and inhibition and the children come very early to distinguish between good and evil, right and wrong. It is worthy of note that most children respond very favorably to the new form of dignity resulting from power to choose and act upon a choice. This self-discipline is most effective and prevents the confusion of goodness with immobility and badness with activity which occurs in many schools.

3. *The principle of independence.* This is a basic consideration since the child needs this in order to be free. A child might take longer than others to wash, dress, and feed himself or assemble certain blocks and letters—and he might not even do these things well—but he must be allowed to do them with as little help as necessary so that he can act for himself, become independent, self-controlled, and responsible.

4. *The principle of respect for authority and intelligent*

obedience. Montessori observed that a child normally passes through three stages. In the first period, a child is too underdeveloped to understand. The second period occurs when the desire to obey and the motor power of execution are partially formed. The third period begins when the child desires and is able to respond at once. His sense of power grown, the child takes pride in the accomplishment of freely chosen and independent acts and loves to prove that he is able to respond. This final stage, in which desire, knowledge, and ability are balanced, is reached very slowly, so that what we often call willfulness is in reality a condition of an undisciplined will. Here the principle of respect for authority and intelligent obedience must be preserved if an effective learning experience is to take place.

5. *The principle of the lack of necessity of rewards and punishments.* Montessori felt such external inducements were not necessary because human powers function spontaneously in a proper environment and delight in their own inherent functioning. Natural satisfaction, then, is its own best motive and reward. Prizes merely put another motive first so that the child is not trained to find pleasure in the work but in an outside reward. Montessori, however, did distinguish between expression of approval and prizes; she advocated verbal encouragement stemming from a sympathetic relationship since this brought joy in the child's accomplishment.

In placing these five principles into practice in her *Casa dei Bambini,* Maria Montessori removed the obstacles of the adult environment from the classroom. There was no teacher's desk, and the equipment of the classroom was made proportionate to the size and strength of the children. Special furnishings and utensils, reduced in size, such as tables, chairs, washbasins, cabinets, etc., were used in the classroom because the children must be free to live in their own little world.

But more than mere furnishings, the "prepared environment" consisted of the special materials through which the children could develop their potentialities to the fullest. Since the materials used were self-corrective, the children could evaluate the outcomes with no intervention and, in effect, teach themselves. Such an atmosphere tends to make the children want to learn. The materials themselves have a high sensory appeal—colorful buttoning and lacing frames, rods varying in length, fabrics of differing shades of color, geometric forms, sandpaper alphabets and numbers, and counting boxes and beads were only some of the materials used.

The same objects were used as the child passed from the sensory to the intellectual learning, but with a difference in point of view of which even the child is not aware. This may be illustrated by reading, writing, and the use of numbers.

Writing generally comes first. A younger child learns the muscular control necessary for using writing implements by coloring in outlines which he has made by tracing geometric forms. As he becomes more accurate at this skill, large sandpaper letters are then introduced. The child traces the outline of a letter with his fingers and is given the phonic sound of the letter. This forms an association of visual, tactile, muscular, and auditory senses. Letters making up words are given in the same way. At some time, perhaps age four or five, the child realizes that these symbols can be reproduced and, under his own initiative, he begins to write.

Initially, such words are disconnected and without logical thought. Usually several months go by before children who are writing realize that words may be put together to transmit an idea. When the child has had sufficient practice in writing words, the teacher may write simple commands on a slip of paper such as, "If you can read this, open the window." He makes no effort to help the child to understand, and often it is several days before the youngster can make the proper association. But, all of a sudden, the secret is out! Without a single word being spoken, one human being can communicate with another in this new and mysterious way. In this manner, the children discover the essence of writing and respond to it as eagerly as to a game.

In learning arithmetic, the children first became accustomed to using numbers in a concrete way. Montessori used what she called the "long stair" which was composed of a set of rectangular bars, the longest of which was a meter and the shortest a decimeter, all divided into lengths of a decimeter by alternating red and blue colors. Later, strings of ten beads came into use. With such implements the children can actually see the numbers. They can see addition, subtraction, multiplication, and division. Counting boxes are used, too; in these the correct number of colored sticks are placed into various boxes labeled with that number. The children work with these sensible objects until the essence of the rule becomes absolutely clear to them. Then they begin to work with the numbers alone. The children are able also to learn algebra and square and cube roots at an earlier age than in the traditional schools.

To attempt a portrayal of a Montessori lesson in this section would actually be a repetition of what has been set forth in the preceding paragraphs. Basically, there is no difference between the manner in which Maria Montessori practiced her method and the way it is practiced today. The method itself is modern in that it is a product of the twentieth century.

Actually, no book can formally set down a direct analysis of the objects and their accompanying procedure, as Dr. Montessori herself would counsel, because the various materials and devices must be adapted to the particular environment of the children of the locality in which the school is established.

It is possible to break down the format of this method

to (1) selection of object by individual child; (2) explanation by the teacher of activity necessary to use this object; and (3) independent practice of the rule or skill by the child. Nevertheless, such a division is useless unless a teacher fully understands and abides by the five principles upon which the method is based. In this Montessori approach, the tangible techniques or devices merely aid the teaching process; the vital set of principles makes it possible.

SUMMARY

After a period of great enthusiasm when the Montessori method was new, and after a long period of declining interest in this country, the Whitby School opened in Greenwich, Connecticut, in 1958 under the direction of Nancy McCormick Rambusch. Since that time there has been a startling revival in interest in Montessori's method. It has been estimated that almost one hundred schools of this type have been opened in less than a decade. In view of this revival, particular note should be taken of the hazards as well as the potentialities of this teaching procedure.

Fundamentally, the disadvantages are not many, but they are crucial. The system as advocated by Montessori was only intended for preschool and elementary school children. Hence it has never been adapted to those beyond the first few grades. The second major limitation, particularly relevant in a society which attempts to school all of its members, is the fact that the Montessori method practically demands an individual teacher for each child. The cost, consequently, becomes prohibitive if the method is to be allowed to operate as it should in theory. This is one reason why there are so few schools of this type and almost all of them are small private ventures.

It must be remembered also that there are an insufficient number of teachers properly prepared and with the necessary attributes to work in a school which is permissive and yet demanding in its role. Since the teacher is vitally important in the Montessori method, the lack of qualified staff would seriously handicap the effectiveness of this type of school even if there were sufficient funds for the facilities.

The advantages of the Montessori method, however, are numerous and can be summarized under the one clarification: If properly carried out, this method is highly successful. This pragmatic test of success was demonstrated dramatically by Montessori herself when some of her mentally retarded pupils did better in academic work than their normal fellows. Although she never claimed that her method would make children more intelligent, she did feel that her methods would provide a wider experience at an earlier age. As a result, the children were permitted to develop their talents and skills more fully while still young. They were also more receptive to new learnings than conventionally educated children.

Many authors contend that Montessori's greatest contribution was not her five principles, the devices, or even the "prepared environment," but the individualization of instruction. This aspect of the method, of course, is as old as education itself. The Montessori method in totality, however, is far removed from the ancient and medieval types of tutorial teaching. How closely attuned it is with the demands and needs of the space age is a question which only the future can answer.

19. THE CASE-STUDY METHOD

Let us imagine that this is the real situation.

When John F. Kennedy was a young Senator convalescing from a spinal operation in 1954 and 1955, he wrote a Pulitzer Prize-winning history, *Profiles in Courage.* In this inspiring work, Kennedy presented eight stirring stories about the heroism of some of his predecessors in the United States Senate.

Although this book was adapted into a television series, it is difficult to imagine that this subsequent use was visualized by our late President at the time he wrote the volume. Nevertheless, in written or in dramatic form, *Profiles in Courage* eventually influenced millions. As such, it has been an excellent illustration of what we call a "case study" because it is a collection of particulars presented as part of a general principle.

The format of *Profiles in Courage* is contemporary in its appeal, but it is not new. The narration of incidents to indicate a moral has been a living method of instruction since the time that history was first recorded. Aesop's *Fables,* while concerned with imaginary events and conversations among animals, can be regarded as case studies. Another ancient example of the pedagogical purpose which is inherent in this method is seen in Plutarch's *Lives,* even though this work is not the best according to the modern rules of historiography.

It was not until about 1870, however, that the use of cases was formally advocated as an actual teaching approach. Professor Christopher Langdell at Harvard Law School recommended case studies as the best method of teaching law. As a result, this system has not only become the predominant method used in the law schools of this country today, but it is also important in medicine, sociology, business, administration, and education. In all of these fields, the word "case" may have a slightly different connotation; however, the teaching and the studying in each of these fields are usually connected with the examination of a large number of specific cases. From these particulars, the future lawyer, doctor, social worker, businessman, administrator, or teacher critically examines an authoritative rule and draws valuable generalizations.

The doctor or sociologist uses case studies as a part of his daily work. A patient's case history, which includes a set of symptoms, a prescribed treatment, and a result, is part of the jargon familiar to the entire medical staff. Without this very practical working tool, it would be hard for us to understand how there could be a continuity of treatment. But even if these case histories are developed into articles, they still possess only illustrative value. They assist the medical student or current practitioner in recognizing particular diseases, but they prove something only when a whole series of cases yield satisfactory conclusions. Sometimes a single, careful case study in medicine, with a highly controlled environment, can be extremely valuable when a specific effect can be isolated.

A student in law school encounters a modification of the use of the case study. As a matter of fact, the case studies in law are usually collections of the official authoritative decisions. The courts have applied one or more rules to a set of facts available for observation. The student's first task is to discover what decision has been rendered; more importantly, he must then learn to generalize on the habits of judges in applying or formulating basic rules or principles of decision. The aspiring lawyer soon realizes that predictability is limited in his field. The predictive value is limited because social trends enter into the judicial decision-making process in addition to the variations caused by the diverse personalities of the judges involved. Still the advice which the lawyer will give to his clients is dependent upon his knowledge of particular cases in the past.

At the close of World War I the Graduate School of Business Administration at Harvard University also began to utilize cases. The cases in the field of business are not decisions from a recognized authority, as in medicine and law, but merely descriptions of the behavior of individuals or groups when faced with problems. Whether the student analyzes what the individual corporation officer did or the way a whole company acted in view of a set of circumstances, the net result is still the same—the cases can be classified as cases in decision making. This technique had great success at Harvard and was later adopted by many other graduate business schools.

Following World War II, the Graduate School of Public Administration at Harvard revised its curriculum and began to gather cases, using records of Congressional hearings and other suitable documents about public administration as background for their cases. As with case work in all fields, careful attention was given to the comprehensive, objective, and accurate compilation of the data relating to the areas of concern. Getting the facts straight is always the crucial preliminary to the successful use of the case study.

It is only after the details—the who, what, when, and where—have been explored with insight that a student can attempt to discover the whys and wherefores of the cases. Principles, judgments, and reasons now become the center of discussion as the student attempts to analyze why a certain outcome resulted or how a certain situation might have been prevented from occurring.

This giving to the students an opportunity to discuss principles in practice—whether they agree or disagree—is the essential learning value of the case-study method of teaching. Superficial knowledge or guessing is inadequate, as is satisfaction with one course of action. Alternatives must be seen and weighed because indeed there is rarely one right answer. The goal is not a certain formula or set response. Each case must be evaluated on its own merits or complications, and principles must be synthesized and adapted. Above all, the student should determine why he would support or reject a certain course of action if such a case were his to decide.

"What would you have done in a case like this?" How often in our educational experience have we been asked this question by a perceptive teacher who wanted us to project ourselves into the topic under consideration! Whether we were trying to determine the value of a treaty in social studies, the proper procedure in etiquette, or how to dress for a rainy day, we were called upon to apply some principles we had learned to a concrete set of facts. A common technique in reading classes today is to direct the pupils to read a certain passage about ordinary events in which the main character formulates certain ideas or actions crucial to the plot. In discussing the story after the reading, the teacher then asks the students' opinions of the character's actions or ideas.

Such attempts to analyze thoughts or deeds are elementary modifications of the case-study method. In reading *Profiles in Courage,* for example, students may or may not decide that Daniel Webster's action was prudent in respect to their own individual principles and training.

To employ the case-study method to its fullest advantage, however, the students must be highly specialized and thoroughly schooled in many aspects of their fields. It is for this reason that the pure case-study method is utilized most effectively in graduate and professional schools. The investigation of specific cases gives the students practice in decision making and an opportunity to try out the judgments which will be expected of their particular fields. The necessity of studying cases and theorizing about discipline problems or methodology is as vital to a young teacher as the understanding and citing of judicial precedents is to a young lawyer. An intern certainly would not be expected to make decisions about the advisability of surgery without first investigating many previous records detailing similar situations.

With a fundamental understanding of the value and applicability of case-study learning, the procedure is not difficult. It might be well first to make the distinction between actually compiling the data for a case and using that material for learning. The precise recording of behavior or events on a daily or weekly basis is often practiced by teachers, doctors, or psychiatrists in the observation and study of a particular person. Although frequently referred to as a "case study" in education, such a compilation of facts is not an inherent part of the method now under consideration. It is the genuine use—by experts or novices—of such data reported in each "case" which constitutes the basic methodology.

A series of four steps might serve as a general guideline.

1. *Selection.* Because no class can peruse all cases on record, the teacher must carefully choose the most representative and comprehensive ones. A problem offering many facets or ramifications for varied interpretations is often most functional. The case should also be a good example of the particular points with which a teacher wishes to have the students gain experience. Future school administrators

might consider, "Should Communism be taught in the public schools?"

2. *Reading.* A complete reading of the records of the case selected is required of everyone in the class. Sometimes two or three readings are necessary for a thorough understanding of all the events and their implications.

3. *Analysis.* During or after his reading, each student is advised to break down the case point by point. Why was each action taken? On what principles was a judgment based? Was this decision a wise one for this case? These and other questions must be used by a student in examining the features of each case. Often it is advisable to write down definite comments or opinions.

4. *Discussion.* With individual evaluation of the case complete, it is now time for the members of the class to exchange orally their conclusions or judgments about the case. The teacher, who must know the case thoroughly, frequently may question certain students, always requesting them to support their decisions with principles and rules. Each student may report a different conclusion on the case, but if each view is solidly based on acceptable convictions and tenets of the profession, all may be judged prudent decisions.

Small discussion groups in a seminar-type setting are most conducive to effective case-study work. Because it seeks to have the student project his standards into a practical case, the procedure is a highly subjective and personalized form of study. The more thought the student puts into the problem, the more insight and learning he is apt to gain. In addition, the class interchange enriches and amplifies individual ideas and encourages respect for well-supported alternative decisions, which will always be encountered in professional situations.

SUMMARY

Competency in dealing with real life and practical problems is not easily developed from books or lectures. We usually derive the most from the mistakes—and achievements—of ourselves and others. It is for this reason that the case-study method is of inestimable value to those training for service in a professional capacity.

The case-study technique not only provides experience in decision making and stimulates conceptualization on an individual basis, but it also encourages spirited discussion and interaction for the group.

Of course, such a complete analysis and projective effort require a great deal of time and a teacher of exceptional insight and understanding. Not only must the teacher know the case thoroughly, but he should also be familiar with the needs and backgrounds of his students.

For the ideal use of a case study, the students also must know their field and be well grounded in fundamental principles of action. If these qualifications are met, the case-study method can impart very productive and necessary learning experiences to young people eager to set principles into practice.

20. COMMUNIST METHODS

Are they better than we are?

On October 4, 1957, an eerie beep-beeping was transmitted to radio receivers throughout the world from a small steel ball shooting through space at about 15,000 miles per hour. Sputnik I had been launched and the whole world was impressed.

In these days of astronauts, cosmonauts, men walking in outer space, soft landings on the moon, and rocket landings on Venus, it is difficult for us to recall the impact of Sputnik I's phenomenal achievement. At the time, however, Congressmen called for immediate investigations and almost everyone blamed our educational system for our failure to be first. Even though the study of science had already been idolized, it seemed to laymen (and to many educators) that there was not enough emphasis on science in our schools.

It is true that we in the United States had grown complacent about our educational system and tended to look down our collective noses at the backward peoples of the world. We had even included in this category the Russian people, whom we had considered an illiterate people at the time of the October Revolution of 1917. To say the least, our complacency was suddenly shattered by Sputnik I of October 1957.

What had happened in the intervening forty years since

the establishment of the United Soviet Socialist Republic? How had the Soviets accomplished so much in such a short time? Article 121 of the Constitution of the USSR declares that every citizen has the right to an education. These are some of the principles on which the school system in the Soviet Union is based:

1. All schools and other educational establishments belong to the State. They are all founded and financed by the State.

2. All schools belong to a single unified system with consecutive stages of public education.

3. Education is open to everybody, irrespective of race, color, and religious views, but by a decree of the Council of the People's Commissars of January 21, 1918, all schools and other educational and cultural units are secular and religion is excluded from the curriculum.

4. Education is compulsory and universal. In 1930 four years of school were required; in 1949 this was made seven years. In 1956 the attempt was made to require ten years but this has not yet been a total success. School is held for six days a week.

5. Close contact is maintained between schools and other educational and public organizations, such as the Young Communist League, and trade unions.

Through these fundamental principles, the Soviet schools pursue the goal of fostering the all-around development of the rising generation. All pupils should possess knowledge based on a scientific, materialistic outlook. Since the schools assist in developing this communistic approach to work and social property, the aims and purposes of Communist education are pursued at all stages of schooling, modified according to the age of the pupils.

According to the Communist view, mathematics develops the method of dialectical thinking in pupils, while physics teaches that the material world exists objectively and provides a materialistic explanation of such phenomena as radioactivity and atomic energy. Geology answers questions regarding the creation of the universe, and biology gives a genuinely scientific and materialistic interpretation of the natural development of the organic world.

But what difference do all these theories make in the methodology in Soviet schools? In other words, what methods are used in this land of 210 million people? Is it the method which makes the difference? To answer the last question first, the reply must be in the negative. There seems to be no essential difference between Soviet methods and American methods. As a matter of fact, teachers in Soviet schools are encouraged to use progressive methods.

The dogmatic verbal methods used so frequently prior to the Communist Revolution of 1917 have been supplanted by new methods which aim at stimulating self-activity on the part of the pupils and developing their powers of observation and independent thinking. The project and group methods became popular, and practical work is another aspect of Soviet training. Thus the Soviets have used the same methods as the Americans since the 1917 Revolution.

Under Stalin, the Central Committee on September 5, 1931, ordered that revised programs be introduced by January 1, 1932. A uniform curriculum was established for separate subjects, and courses with clearly defined content were to be mastered by all pupils. More than that, the teacher's individual authority was to be recognized and self-government by the children was required so that their energies would be directed toward strengthening school discipline. The same Central Committee decree of 1931 condemned the project method as leading to the destruction of the school.

A new decree was necessary in August, 1932, to give an explanation of the new method deemed appropriate for Soviet schools. Essentially, this was a socialized recitation method with a given group of pupils following a strict schedule of studies.

Elementary schools in Russia are for children between

the ages of seven and eleven. Throughout the four years all subjects are taught by the same teacher. Not only do these schools teach more science and mathematics than corresponding American schools, but they also present a greater amount of literature, history, geography, and foreign languages. Large sections of the basic readers are devoted to the virtues of Communism; Lenin is read after the child has been in the school for only a few months. The method of teaching reading is based upon a phonics approach, even though Russian is not a perfectly phonetic language.

The fact that the Soviet schools use the same teacher throughout the first four years cannot be classified as a different method; rather it is a different organizational pattern from that which is found in the United States now that we no longer have the one-room schoolhouse. Similarly, some teachers in the United States do advocate and use the phonics approach in teaching reading.

The major difference between Soviet schools and American schools seems to be that the former insist upon a heavier academic load. Although the Soviet news agency Tass recently announced that a course in the theory and history of chess is now being presented at Moscow University, the Soviets tend to avoid the frill subjects for which academic credit is given at some American colleges: ballroom dancing, fly casting, double tumbling, and water skiing.

The success of the Soviet schools might be compared to the success in the training of seminarians as future priests. Since the seminarians frequently live a communal life, the analogy is not too farfetched. Whereas the seminarians are highly motivated to attain their goal of the priesthood, the pupils in a Soviet school are spurred on because their future depends upon their scholastic attainments and adherence to the party line. Hence, the teacher does not have to invoke sanctions or ask for attention; the pupils are already anxious to learn. The young Communist is preparing himself to serve the state just as much as the young seminarian is readying himself to serve the people as a priest. The teacher's task is thus greatly simplified and almost any method can be successful under these conditions.

Since there are no fundamental differences between Soviet and American methods of instruction, we will turn to another Communist country. Embracing over 3,750,000 square miles of territory, Red China includes a population of about 700,000,000 people.

The Communists came to power in China in 1949. The educational policy specifies that the education in People's China is to be national, scientific, and popular in character. The Chinese Communist aim is to raise the cultural level of the people, particularly workers and peasants, by equipping them "intellectually, morally, ideologically, and technically" to become constructive citizens of the new socialist state.

There is a close link between theory and practice which leads to the avoidance of all attempts to stuff the children's minds by recitation, memory work, and other formalistic methods. Pupils are therefore encouraged to ask questions and review what they have learned. Teachers generally use the visual method, taking objects and practical illustrations to explain a subject, and organize pupils to undertake experiments, educational visits, and other projects. Consequently, methods in Mainland China are no different from the teaching methods employed in the Soviet Union. Frequently there is a large lecture given and the lecturer is provided with a teaching assistant who may very well be serving the Party's purpose of checking on the lecturer's orthodoxy.

At the collegiate level or the teacher-training level, political education is frequently carried out by means of small group discussions. In these groups of ten to twelve students, self-criticism is encouraged. In this way the regime keeps itself informed about the inner thoughts of others and maintains control. Each group has a leader who is either a member of the Communist Party or a member of its affiliate, the New Democratic Youth League. As a result, students are kept constantly aware of the current party line.

However, the available evidence forces us to conclude that there is no substantial difference in methods of teaching between those used by the Communists in China and those used in our schools in the United States.

SUMMARY

After this cursory examination of the complex world that lies behind the Iron and Bamboo Curtains, the American citizen still wants to know why the Communist systems have been so successful in promoting scientific and political advances. It could be pointed out that in an earlier day our national survival was not so attributed to the schools. When Andrew Jackson defeated Sir Edward Pakenham on the morning of January 8, 1815 in the Battle of New Orleans, no one gave credit to the schools. Perhaps the lack of schooling had helped the American cause.

But the twentieth century has seen the introduction of radio, television, radar, sonar, electronic computers, the automobile, the airplane, and the motorization of just about everything from toothbrushes to children's games. Consequently today's society expects a causal relationship between quantity of schooling and mechanical progress. The Soviet Union has certainly made education its "grand passion." Perhaps the difference is that the Russian and Chinese Communists have concentrated their energies on an increase in scientific advances, while the Americans have poured most of their resources into an increase in living comforts.

In any event, the investigation which has been conducted gives no evidence of a substantial difference in methods, nor does it provide us with any unique method of teaching.

21. BE AN ARTIST!

An artist, to most people, is a painter like Michelangelo or Leonardo da Vinci. In the true sense, however, every good teacher is also an artist.

Michelangelo proved that he mastered his art by painstakingly painting the ceiling of the Sistine Chapel. Slowly and carefully, he worked day after day for four years, using many tools and brushes and a diversity of colors, shades, and shapes in depicting his classic panorama. Leonardo's *Mona Lisa* was also created with precision and technical virtuosity. Even though the smiling lady was but a single subject, the painter likewise had to blend many different pigments and varied brush strokes to achieve his finished portrait.

A variety of shape, color, tool, brush, and tone—this is all part of the blend that produces the artistry which can enrich the lives of men. So it is with teaching—perfection is reached only by a combination of many methods, devices, techniques, and shades of interpretation. Just as a great artist could never produce a masterpiece by adhering to a set of numbered patterns or by using one stroke or one color, so also good teachers could never be satisfied with one method or one approach to the art of teaching.

It has been said that variety adds spice to life; we might

also say that variety adds spice and pleasing flavor to classroom learning. No one enjoys change more than the younger generation. The very fads they start in the food world are the strongest indication of their delight in variety.

So it is with the intellectual and educational development of our children. Variety remains the spice of life, and the teaching craftsman is never content until he develops a great repertoire of methods, techniques, and procedures for the production of his art.

Besides the methods described in this book, there are others which might best suit a specific class at a particular time. The simultaneous method of St. John Baptist de la Salle, the Ursuline method of St. Angela Merici, the Munich method of Kerchenstiener or the Stieglitz method, the Salesian method of Don Bosco, the Sulpician method of Jean Jacques Olier, the team-teaching method, the use of teaching machines and programmed learning as advocated by B. F. Skinner, or the audiovisual method of television and motion pictures are among those not included here. Basically, all of these methods are either extensions or combinations of the fundamental principles and methodological approaches which have been analyzed, and it would therefore be somewhat repetitious to reoutline such common areas. Besides, a good teacher will automatically synthesize and shape different methods to fit a certain teaching situation whether he is familiar with two, four, or forty different methods.

It is axiomatic, then, that method per se is not a guarantee of the quality of instruction. No single method will insure good teaching; in fact, a method which produces artistic teaching under one set of circumstances may give poor results under different circumstances.

A method of teaching is a means to an end; in itself, the method is neutral in the same way that dynamite is neutral. The explosive may be used to level ground for a highway or to blow up a safe. Similarly, methods of teaching can be used to teach men how to get to heaven or how to enslave the world. The success of a method, therefore, depends largely on the personal gifts and characteristics of the teacher—the artisan.

To be a good teacher, a person must know his subject, the capacity of his pupil, and be able to communicate with his pupil. The method he chooses is the means to establish this essential communication.

The success of this formula was proven by the experience of Anna, the English school teacher depicted in *The King and I*. Anna's knowledge of her subject could not be doubted, but her proficiency in teaching was derived from her ability to communicate meaningfully with her pupils. She saw them as individuals and she adapted herself to their ways in order to achieve her goals. This is true of all good teaching; such artisans use a variety of methods and find no single one a panacea. Good teachers adapt methods to the purpose, content, pupil level and their own particular ability.

So it was with the venerable Mr. Chips in James Hilton's marvelous novel and with Maria Von Trapp in *The Sound of Music*. Even Henry Higgins succeeded in *My Fair Lady*, although he overemphasized the memorization method, because he possessed the knowledge of his subject and was able to obtain the intelligent cooperation of Eliza Doolittle. He also used the different techniques and devices of the lecture, discussion, and Socratic questioning styles of teaching.

Like Anna, Mr. Chips, Maria Trapp and Henry Higgins, a teacher is often naturally endowed and able to make his presentation in an appealing fashion. It is the author's hope that this volume can help those who are already thus endowed to learn new techniques, and those who are not so blessed to discover the best ways of communicating what they have learned themselves.

The need for good teachers is greater than ever before. It is a standard proverb that man without learning is like the soil untilled. In today's world, no pupil's mind should be left uncultivated.

To accept this challenge, the teacher must practice his craft with the same skill as a Michelangelo or a Leonardo. Education must never be reduced to a single set of unvarying laws or rules of procedure which anyone can master if he just reads the directions. The assembly line must be left to industry.

Teaching is nothing less than the vibrant contact of one mind with another mind. And that is an art.

Be an artist . . . And so teach!

A BEGINNING BIBLIOGRAPHY

There are today comparatively few worthwhile general works on methods of teaching. A detailed chapter-by-chapter summary of pertinent references would therefore seem to be of dubious value to the student. In place of the customary listings, however, there are some sources which can be recommended for the study of particular methods and the men who advocate them. This appendix is but a start on the long road to further examination and evaluation by the reader.

As a beginning, an overall view of most of the methods discussed in this book can be found in the excellent volume by John S. Brubacher, *The History of the Problems of Education,* 2nd edition (New York: McGraw-Hill Book Company, 1966) in which two chapters are devoted to methodology as one of the key problems in education.

Specifically, it is undoubtedly best for the reader to examine thoroughly the works of authors who inaugurated a method in order to absorb as much of the spirit as well as the specific techniques of the founder. In this regard, Robert S. Ulich's *Three Thousand Years of Educational Wisdom* (Cambridge, Mass.: Harvard University Press, 1954) is particularly valuable since it is a collection of readings of the original documents of many of the world's outstanding educators.

A deeper insight into the lecture and discussion methods can be gained from the many studies listed in the *Educational Index;* these studies often contrast the lecture and discussion methods as to their effectiveness, and there is extensive research reported in the literature with varying conditions imposed. One such instructive article on the lecture method is that by John N. Marr, Dean W. Plath, John H. Wakely, and Donald M. Wilkins, "The Contribution of the Lecture to College Teaching," *Journal of Educational Psychology,* 1960, Vol. LI, pp. 277–284.

For a genuine appreciation of the Socratic approach, there is nothing better than a reading of the Platonic dialogs. Similarly, the most comprehensive way to gain an adequate understanding of the parable method is by studying the original narratives in the Gospels. Nevertheless, Leonard Nelson's *Socratic Method and Critical Philosophy* (New York: Dover Publications, Inc., 1965, paper) is recommended as a source of added dimension in Socratic interpretation, as is James A. Jordan Jr.'s "Socratic Teaching" in the *Harvard Educational Review,* XXXIII (Winter, 1963), pp. 96-104. Msgr. Ronald Knox and Rev. Ronald Cox, C.M., have also done much to elucidate the method of the parable in their *The Gospel Story* (New York: Sheed and Ward, 1944).

The Dominicans are the best translators of their revered forebear, St. Thomas Aquinas, and the assiduous student is urged to peruse not only the entire *Summa Theologica* (New York: Benziger Brothers, 1948) but also the *Summa Contra Gentiles* (London: Burns, Oates and Washbourne, Ltd., 1924). A commentary about the scholastic method can be found in *Universities of Europe in the Middle Ages* (Oxford: Clarendon Press, 1936) by Hastings Rashdall, while Gilbert Keith Chesterton's *St. Thomas Aquinas* (New York:

Sheed and Ward, 1954, and Doubleday Image Books, paper) offers penetrating insights into the great scholastic as a man and teacher.

The foremost volumes on the origins of the Jesuit method are Robert Schwickerath's *Jesuit Education* (St. Louis: B. Herder Book Co., 1904), Edward A. Fitzpatrick's *St. Ignatius and the Ratio Studiorum* (New York: McGraw-Hill Book Company, Inc., 1933), and Alan P. Farrell's *The Jesuit Code of Liberal Education* (Milwaukee: Bruce Publishing Co., 1938).

In order to gain a deeper knowledge of St. Vincent de Paul's contributions to education, the principal source of study is the complete edition of his works with biographical notes accompanying the text translated by Rev. Joseph Leonard, C.M., entitled *The Life and Works of St. Vincent de Paul* (Baltimore: The Newman Press, 1953). There have also been many other commentaries on the life of this saint which touch upon his method. One of the most suitable is Msgr. Jean Calvet's *Saint Vincent de Paul,* translated by Lancelot C. Sheppard (New York: David McKay Company, 1948).

John Locke is not a very easy man to understand, since he often contradicts himself. However, the reader who wishes to evaluate Locke's philosophy for himself is referred to *Some Thoughts Concerning Education* (Cambridge: Cambridge University Press, 1880) and "On the Conduct of Understanding" in *The Philosophical Works of John Locke,* edited by J. A. St. John (London: George Bell and Sons, 1905).

Although the original writings of Jean Jacques Rousseau are also hard to follow, the reader is referred to *Émile,* translated by Barbara Foxley (London: J. M. Dent and Sons Ltd., 1911), in order to become familiar with this naturalistic point of view. Attention should also be given to Rousseau's enthusiastic follower, Johann Pestalozzi and his *Leonard and Gertrude,* translated by Eva Channing (Boston: Ginn and Co., 1885) and *How Gertrude Teaches Her Children,* translated by Lucy E. Holland and Francis C. Turner (Syracuse: C. W. Bardeen, 1894) as a proper follow-up in evaluating naturalism in education. A commentator on the methodology of these two men is Adolph E. Meyer in *The Development of Education in the Twentieth Century,* 2nd edition (New York: Prentice-Hall, 1949).

One of the most worthwhile accounts of the monitorial system is probably found in J. F. Reigart's *The Lancasterian System of Instruction in the Schools of New York City* (New York: Columbia University, Teachers College, 1916), but a more meaningful modern account is presented in the *Phi Delta Kappan,* XL, No. 4, January, 1959, pp. 164–167, in which Phil E. Hager gives a fair appraisal of this method's rise and fall, entitled "Nineteenth-Century Experiments with Monitorial Teaching."

The Herbartian Method is revealed most explicitly in the writings of Herbart himself, *The Science of Education,* translated by Henry M. and Emmie Felkin (New York: E. P. Dutton and Co., 1924) and *Outlines of Educational Doctrine,* translated by Alexis F. Lanze (New York: The Macmillan Company, 1901), but the interpreters who made his work more applicable to the American scene were Charles DeGarmo in *Herbart and the Herbartians* (New York: Charles Scribner's Sons, 1896) and Gabriel Compayre in *Herbart and Education by Instruction* (New York: Thomas Y. Crowell and Company, 1907).

To understand John Dewey is a masterful task, but to give this famous educator a fair hearing the reader owes it to himself to examine Dewey's own *Democracy and Education: An Introduction to the Philosophy of Education* (New York: The Macmillan Company, 1963, and Free Press Paperbacks) and *How We Think* (New York: D. C. Heath, 1910).

William Heard Kilpatrick's project method is described most thoroughly in his *Foundations of Method* (New York: The Macmillan Company, 1925). Similarly, a reader interested in the unit plan is referred to Henry C. Morrison's *The Practice of Teaching in the Secondary School* (Chicago: The University of Chicago Press, 1931).

The socialized recitation method is well explained in Herbert F. A. Smith's *Secondary School Teaching: Modes for Reflective Thinking* (Dubuque: Wm. C. Brown Company, 1964) and in *Modern Secondary Education* (New York: Rinehart and Company, Inc., 1959) by William M. Alexander and J. Galen Saylor.

Maria Montessori, despite her many commentators, is still the best source for a mastery of her particular technique in *The Montessori Method*, translated by Anne E. George (New York: Frederick A. Stokes Co., 1919, and New York: Schocken Books, paper).

The case-study method can be investigated by several different avenues. One of the best roads to follow, in the opinion of this author, is Bruno Lasker's *Democracy Through Discussion* (New York: The H. W. Wilson Co., 1949). The *Handbook of Group Discussion* by Russell P. Wagner and Carroll C. Arnold (Boston: Houghton Mifflin, 1950), and Harold P. Zelko's *Successful Conferences and Discussion Techniques* (New York: McGraw-Hill Book Company, 1957, paper) are fairly typical of volumes designed to assist discussion leaders. Harold Stein has written an excellent introduction to the use of cases in the volume he edited entitled *Public Administration and Policy Development: A Case Book* (New York: Harcourt, Brace and Company, 1952).

Communist methods are difficult to discover in the literature. Descriptions are quite vague and general; even those who have spent a long time in investigating conditions in Soviet Russia and Red China do not devote much space in reporting on specific methodologies.

Other volumes which can help teachers improve their techniques in teaching are many and varied. Especially recommended are Gilbert Highet's *The Art of Teaching* (New York: Vintage paperback, 1963) and Harry N. Rivlin's *Teaching Adolescents in Secondary Schools; the Principles of Effective Teaching in Junior and Senior High Schools,* 2nd edition (New York: Appleton-Century-Crofts, 1961).

INDEX